God Is Gracious

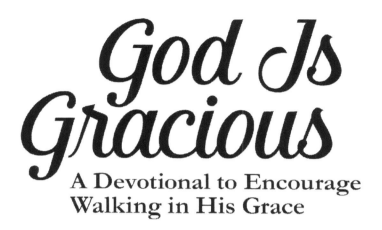

JOANN NISLY

Forewords by: Gary & Marilyn Damron
Julian & Bertha Nisly

First Printing: 2016

ISBN-13: 978-0-692-66663-0

Joann Nisly
PO Box 103
Partridge, Kansas 67566

www.nislysHOPEministries.com

For more books, visit www.nislybooksales.com.

DEDICATION

This book is dedicated to God, Who has been so gracious in walking with me on my journey. Even when I didn't understand His great love, He pursued me in His gentle way. I'm thankful for His Son, Jesus, who came to show us the Father, exemplifying unconditional love and grace for all!

CONTENTS

God's Grace Demonstrated Through Communication

God's Grace Demonstrated in the Daily Grind

God's Grace Demonstrated in Strongholds

God's Grace Demonstrated When Life Is Difficult

God's Grace Demonstrated Through Forgiveness

God's Grace Demonstrated Through Encouragement

ACKNOWLEDGMENTS

I have been so thankful for the people who have impacted me on my journey of healing and understanding God and the way He works. I am still on that journey. Over the last twelve years there have been numerous people who have been encouragers for me through some dark valleys. More recently there has been a group of supporters for my husband and I as we established HOPE Ministries of Kansas, a Biblical counseling facility. My husband and various friends have entered into the vision of seeing this book come to pass and it has made the process enjoyable. Without the help of the following people, this book would have never been possible. I'm thankful to God for each of them.

I would like to express appreciation to:

My husband, Nevin, who gave me freedom to spend the time to write this book. His continuous support and encouragement was a blessing. He showed interest and offered suggestions as he faithfully read each chapter. He has walked with me in the journey of applying the principles talked about in this book to our marriage. We are excited to see growth and change happening in our lives.

My parents, Morris and Norma Ropp, who gave of themselves to raise me in a Christian home. They passed on to me an interest to serve on the mission field and have been supportive of me throughout all my years. I am very grateful for the heritage of a strong faith in Christ as well as their unending prayers for me.

Don and Marilyn Showalter, founders of Hearts Alive!, who walked with me as friends, counselors and mentors during some very difficult years of depression. They offered much encouragement and friendship, pointing me to Jesus. Marilyn was often available for phone chats and inspired me to keep on the journey. When she passed away in 2013, I grieved the loss of a dear friend and mentor.

Allen and Carolyn Miller, who were also my counselors for several years, leading me to Jesus for continued emotional healing. They spent time with Nevin and me for our premarital counseling. Their belief in me, their incredible patience, and continued friendship and interest in my life are things for which I thank God.

The HOPE Ministries Board, who has offered much support and guidance in our ministry. They are Arlen and Gloria Mast, Gene Miller, Lynn and Sandra Miller, Ray and Gina Miller, and Julian and Bertha Nisly all living in our local community in Kansas. They have also shown personal interest in us. When I told them about writing this book, they were unanimously behind the idea, giving encouragement along the way.

John and Barb Regier, founders of Caring for the Heart Ministries, who had vision to provide a Biblical model of leading people to Jesus. Because of this model of counseling, I have a whole new outlook on life. Many of the concepts I learned from Caring for the Heart are woven into this book. Nevin and I also have enjoyed personal counseling with John and our marriage has been enriched because of those opportunities, as well as from the training we received under him.

Gary and Marilyn Damron, who have become friends and mentors for us in the last few years. They have provided ongoing support, love and encouragement to us as a couple. Their willingness to proof each of these chapters, offering ideas and encouragement, has been a huge blessing. We are thankful for their contribution to our lives.

My sister, Debora Ropp, who has given much time in reading and proofing different chapters of this book, offering suggestions and encouragement. She, along with the rest of my family, offered prayers and support to me during my journey through depression.

Gina Miller, Bertha Nisly, and Joanna Yoder, who all gave sacrificially of their time to read these chapters offering advice, interest and encouragement to me along the way. I am thankful for the friendship of each of these ladies and the contributions they have made to my life.

My niece, Tracia Ropp, who gave time and expertise in designing the front cover and assisting with the formatting of the book.

And especially God, who gave me vision for this book and has been faithful in extending His gracious gift of healing to my heart.

FOREWORDS

God Is Gracious is a devotional book that goes straight to the heart. You will get a glimpse of Joann's life and her journey of healing. Her honesty and sincerity are refreshing, and she is able to put words to the many struggles of life. In her transparency of sharing her life experiences, it creates a real and honest dialogue that many will relate to. In all of it, she invites Jesus in to show her the answers for her heart that bring healing and peace. There are precious nuggets on every page.

What a privilege it has been getting to know Joann, and her husband, Nevin, over the last few years. It's delightful to see how God has opened up her heart and helped her find answers to everyday problems in life. Joann is a testimony to the power of God's grace and healing. Her willingness to share her deep wounds and the profound effect they've had on her will invite others to look at their own hearts. As she sought God, He has not only met her in her own struggles, but has given practical tools for anyone struggling with the issues of life.

God is using Joann's healing and the freedom she enjoys today to speak hope and life to many hearts. The peace and joy that only Jesus can give comes shining through the pages of this book. May God use it to speak His love and care to your heart.

Gary & Marilyn Damron
Caring for the Heart counselors
March 2016

We came to know Joann and her husband, Nevin, when they moved to our community. We have personally experienced the help they give to couples and individuals through their counseling, and have come to deeply appreciate them and their ministry. Joann has a heart of compassion for those who are struggling and a passion to help others because of her own life experiences. Through our interactions we have grown in our understanding of grace and walking with Jesus in a more personal way.

We are excited at the potential this book has to help people in their journey. We believe it has tools for helping those who are stuck in negative cycles, are hurting, or desire to understand more of God's love and grace. Through Joann's writings you will be encouraged to go deeper in your relationship with God. We trust you will find your heart encouraged through these pages; may it be a way for God to show you more of His character and His care for you.

Julian & Bertha Nisly
Pastor and HOPE Ministries board members
March 2016

INTRODUCTION

This book is not intended to be a magical fix for people, but rather to show the grace of God. I believe that emotional healing comes only from Jesus, the Great Physician, and it is necessary to turn people toward Him. Therefore, prayer must be a major part of the process of healing for a heart. Because of this, with each devotional I have included a prayer. These are only suggestions to help people get started in communicating with Jesus in a personal way. This method of prayer is not often taught and many people find themselves at a loss as to what kinds of questions to ask. It is recommended that one may want to write down the things heard from Jesus. These thoughts will be an encouragement in dark moments. My prayer is that through the use of this book, people will see Jesus in refreshing ways and understand that He is personal, gentle and desires to be involved in their lives. All Scriptures quoted are taken from the New Living Translation unless otherwise noted.

He Giveth More Grace

He giveth more grace as our burdens grow greater,
He sendeth more strength as our labors increase;
To added afflictions He addeth His mercy,
To multiplied trials He multiplies peace.

When we have exhausted our store of endurance,
When our strength has failed ere the day is half done,
When we reach the end of our hoarded resources
Our Father's full giving is only begun.

Fear not that thy need shall exceed His provision,
Our God ever yearns His resources to share;
Lean hard on the arm everlasting, availing;
The Father both thee and thy load will upbear.

His love has no limits, His grace has no measure,
His power no boundary known unto men;
For out of His infinite riches in Jesus
He giveth, and giveth, and giveth again.

Words: Annie Johnson Flint (Public Domain)

God's Grace Demonstrated to a Fallen World

Day 1

ARE ALL PEOPLE REALLY DAMAGED?

"For the wages of sin is death, but the free gift of God is eternal life through Christ Jesus our Lord." Romans 6:23

"...he hath sent me to heal the brokenhearted..." Luke 4:18

In the last several years I have asked myself the question, "How does the death and resurrection of Christ 2000 years ago affect me in my daily life?" This question has motivated me to search and watch for answers to that question.

Why did God send His Son? He came to save us from the wages of sin that came into the world in the Garden of Eden. Did He come only to give the gift of salvation? If that is the only purpose, that means I can do whatever I want since I've accepted that gift. Is it possible that Jesus' death and resurrection has many more effects on our daily lives?

When sin entered the world, conflict and tension also came. It didn't take Adam and Eve long to start the blame game. Then came the consequences of leaving the Garden. Their children had animosity toward each other...and it passed on down. This is what the consequence of sin in the world does: it creates damage in our hearts. This damage affects those around us, whether we are aware of it or not.

Because our damage has always been a part of us, we often don't even see we have problems. Reacting to them becomes an acceptable way to live. Sometimes we don't like some of the things we do, but we don't know how to change them. We find it easier to do what seems "normal" to us. It doesn't really seem necessary to understand more about ourselves. We just try to move forward and do our best to improve.

When a child's heart is damaged, he will develop coping mechanisms to survive life. These coping mechanisms are ways of making life bearable. The trusting, sensitive heart of a child does not know how to process hurt. Unless a caring adult shows them comfort and understanding, coping will be used to reduce the hurt. Healing is not likely to happen, even if it appears that he has adjusted quite well. As an adult, the person may find visiting this damage very painful after having lived out of coping methods for so long.

Some people fear they will be blaming individuals if they talk about how they have been hurt. This fear keeps them stuck in the hurt. Acknowledging hurt and where it comes from is one of the first steps toward healing. If we are always fearful that we are blaming another person, our hearts will never get the attention that God intended.

This is the way the enemy works. He wants to keep us from recognizing his desire to destroy us. As we believe his lies and live from them, he gets a foothold in our lives and convinces us that our reactions are normal. This robs us of the life and purpose that God intended for us to experience. Our focus will stay on ourselves and survival instead of on Jesus and the life He gives. Jesus longs to come into our hurts and bring comfort to us. In doing this He reveals messages that our hearts have believed from past damage. This allows us to recognize how we function from those messages today. Through Jesus' resurrection, He has brought the ability to experience LIFE each day we live. He is the healer of the damage that comes from the consequence of sin in the world!

PRAYER:

Lord Jesus, thank You for saving me from eternal death. Thank You for being a personal Jesus and desiring to heal my broken heart. Lord, is there damage from the past that I have been afraid to visit? How would You like to bring comfort to my heart? What messages have I believed from that hurt? Are there ways that I am hurting people close to me because of messages I've believed from damage as a child? Lord, how does the fact that You died and rose again so long ago affect me today? What would You like to show me about Yourself as I walk through this day?

Day 2

THE RIPPLE EFFECT OF DAMAGE

"The Lord is slow to anger and filled with unfailing love, forgiving every kind of sin and rebellion. But he does not excuse the guilty. He lays the sins of the parents upon their children; the entire family is affected - even children in the third and fourth generations." Numbers 14:18

"All praise to God, the Father of our Lord Jesus Christ. God is our merciful Father and the source of all comfort. He comforts us in all our troubles so that we can comfort others. When they are troubled, we will be able to give them the same comfort God has given us." II Cor. 1: 3-4

The excitement in our home increased as we anticipated the visit of our children and grandchildren. We knew the new puppies would be a hit and many little hands would want to hold the two-week-old little fur balls. We weren't disappointed. Grandpa put a tiny puppy in the hands of our little granddaughter. She was excited to show Grandma and carried the squirming little puppy around the table. Just as the little girl reached me, the puppy toppled out of her hands. I quickly reached out to rescue the falling puppy, exclaiming to her grandpa that he shouldn't have let her carry the puppy alone. The little girl rushed to her mama who was close by and cried.

My reaction that day hurt my granddaughter. My inability to control my fear of the puppy getting hurt caused an inappropriate reaction toward her grandpa. The little girl may have thought it was all her fault that Grandma raised her voice at Grandpa. This was not comforting. In no way did I ever intend to hurt my granddaughter, but I did. I made her afraid. Thankfully I was able to apologize to her and before long she was interacting with me again. Because of the healing Jesus had been doing in my heart, I recognized my reaction as inappropriate and could make it right with our granddaughter, as well as with Nevin (Grandpa). It helped me to see how I can hurt people even when I have no intention of it.

This is often the way it is with parents and other people in authority. They do the best they can, but because of past damage, reactions are learned. These reactions are passed on to the sensitive hearts of children, assuming that the children are unaffected. If passed off, the enemy will use these seemingly "harmless" happenings to plant lies into the hearts of the children. If adults will not address the pain in their own hearts allowing Jesus to comfort their pain, they will react the way they learned to react in their homes. Hurting people will continue to hurt people, creating a ripple effect. Unfortunately, even in Christian circles, people do not see the damage they create. If they are approached, they don't want to admit it because they didn't intend to hurt. Sometimes if they do admit that they did something damaging, they will try to justify it and not make restitution. The heart of the child is missed totally. A perfect opportunity to be "Jesus with skin on" has been overlooked and the child's heart does not experience the comfort that Jesus intended.

If my grandchild was to experience this type of reaction from me on a daily basis, she would learn to cope with it. She would naturally keep her distance from me. She would be afraid of doing something to make me unhappy. She would not feel safe to be alone with me. She probably wouldn't even remember the incident that the enemy used to plant into her mind the message that Grandma is not a safe person. She would grow up knowing that she and Grandma were never close without even understanding why.

God intended for us to enjoy relationship. We were made for relationship. Jesus was an excellent example of caring for people's hearts. As adults we have the opportunity to be a picture of Jesus to those children around us. If we allow Him to comfort our hearts, we will be able to better recognize when others are hurting. We will then be able to pass on that comfort.

PRAYER:

Lord Jesus, are there any ways I have hurt people around me in the last 24 hours? When I react that way, how old do I feel inside? Did something happen to me as a child that causes me to have that reaction? Would You draw me a picture of my hurting heart? Is there anything that keeps me from being able to extend comfort to those around me? Do I find it hard with any particular person, Jesus? Why is that? In the coming days would You show me more about this?

Day 3

WHAT KIND OF FOUNDATION?

"If the foundations be destroyed, what can the righteous do?"
Psalm 11:3 (KJV)

My husband and I returned from a trip and were pleasantly surprised to see the foundation of our new cottage had been poured. This was one of the first steps in fulfilling a dream of having a building to enhance our ministry. Construction on the hospitality cottage took place over the next few months. Within about five months, we began using this cottage. Looking at it, we can't see the foundation upon which the rest of the building was erected. Yet the foundation is an important part.

So it is in our lives. Our past becomes the foundation upon which we live. Because of the damage in the world due to sin, our foundations are often not very stable. We become accustomed to the instability and tend to believe we are built upon a solid foundation--whether it is true or not. There are things in our foundations that are positive. There are also things in our foundations that are negative. It is the negative things that cause cracking and shifting in the foundation. This creates problems in the other parts of the "building."

There are three natural tendencies evident when we have an unstable foundation. Denial of the damage is one of these. Sometimes denial is purposeful and sometimes it is a coping mechanism that young children use to survive. As we grow older, we don't even realize we're in denial. When we live in denial of past hurts and the effects they have on us, we may put pressure on others to also live in denial. It is difficult to understand the feelings of others because we are so numb to our own. Our ability to show compassion out of an open heart is limited.

Justifying our actions is another way of dealing with an unstable foundation. We may look around us and see others doing the same things. We won't be motivated to change because "everyone else is doing it." This brings hurt to those around us. Justification has potential to keep us unknowingly chained to the hurts of our past. When we become accustomed to the hurts we received from others, we may not see that any damage was done to our own hearts. We may tend to justify ourselves when we do the same to others. For example, if we saw anger or frustration demonstrated as an acceptable way of dealing with inconveniences while growing up, it will be normal for us to repeat those same actions to those close to us today. We will do this without awareness of any damage being done. It is an acceptable thing in our minds and we will expect the people around us to "accept us as we are."

Blame is also a common tendency when we have an unhealthy foundation. When we project blame, it's necessary to figure out who is at fault. We will continue to heap blame on others in an effort to keep guilt from settling on ourselves. Blame often develops into bitterness. When we live in blame, we believe that the other person needs to change in order for healing to happen in our own lives. This causes us to stay stuck in our unhealthy reactions and it limits the work of Christ on Calvary. Instead of Jesus being the Great Physician, we are believing the lie that the other person is responsible for our healing. If they don't do their part, we will be stuck in the rut forever.

When Jesus died on the cross, did He really do enough? Did He really pay the necessary penalty for all sin--theirs and mine? Did He really conquer the enemy? Yes, He did! Because of this, He has power over the enemy to heal our damaged hearts and rebuild the unhealthy foundation. Even when other people don't change or recognize how they hurt us, we can invite Him to do a rebuilding of our hearts; He **is** the Master Builder! As He does His continual revision and restoration, we will not keep passing the same unhealthy reactions to the next generation.

PRAYER:

Lord, I'm sure I've become accustomed to my own belief system and my damaged foundation. Has my heart been in denial about any of my past pain? Have I been justifying any of my reactions to people? If so, why do I find it necessary to justify myself? Is there something my heart has been believing that is not true? Lord Jesus, how would You like to change that? Does my heart need healing? Have I been excusing myself by projecting blame on others? What has that looked like in my life, Lord? Would You draw me a picture of blame and how it affects me and others? Jesus, how would You like to restore my heart so I can live with an open heart toward others and pass Your love and compassion onto them?

Day 4

WHERE'S MY FOCUS?

"God's law was given so that people could see how sinful they were. But as people sinned more and more, God's wonderful grace became more abundant. So just as sin ruled over the people and brought them to death, now God's wonderful grace rules instead, giving us right standing with God..." Romans 5:20-21

The student came to school and the homework was not done...again. As the teacher, I believed it was necessary to make sure my students experienced consequences for their wrongdoing. This in itself was not a problem, but too many times, I found myself frustrated at them. In frustration, I focused on how to get rid of the problem rather than focusing on the relationship with the students. Therefore, there were times I missed opportunities to understand what was happening in their hearts. I didn't realize that the things stirring deep within them were causing the disobedience or infractions that were so evident to me. It wasn't abnormal to find the wrongdoing an inconvenience, and my response could be harsh and without grace. It was logical to me that if they knew what was right, they should just do it! Looking back, I did this same thing to myself, having little patience if I found myself struggling over and over in the same area.

I lived out of a twisted belief system. I knew sin must be punished, so I was afraid of doing wrong and the consequence that God was going to mete out to me. Fear of His harshness motivated me to try hard to do the right thing. I wasn't motivated because of His love for me. His love would be present only if I did right. Because this was the thinking in my heart, I had little grace for those around me who did not measure up or put forth the effort in doing right like I thought they should.

Focusing on the problem did not create the heart change that I had anticipated in myself or within my students. It created fear and pressure. What if I would have understood how to focus on what was happening in my own heart? Would have I been able to better understand and give more grace to my students? Jesus cares about the damage in our hearts. This damage can bring confusion to us, paralyze us or rob us of motivation and other things. When there is little understanding for these emotions stirring inside, we will tend to make choices that lead to sin. It is the outward sin that people see and try to "fix." We are not often taught that Jesus longs to heal and comfort that confused, misunderstood or paralyzed heart. The message we get instead is that He is only concerned about our right and wrong actions. Our focus stays on our sins, problems or failures and tends to be what we focus on in other people also. It is easy to forget that the law of God was to show us that we *can't* keep it, but rather that we need the wonderful grace of God.

Too often, healing and restoration are only connected to cleansing from sin. Rather than focusing on people's sin, Jesus looked deeper. He did not shake His finger at Zaccheus, throw a stone at the adulterous woman, or criticize Peter. He accepted them where they were, cared about them, and understood their hurting hearts and each of them was drawn to Him.

As people walked with me on my emotional journey, they didn't focus on my negative attitude, critical spirit and bitterness. They helped me understand that I had a heart that was hurting and led me to Jesus to receive comfort for it. I experienced His love, grace, healing and comfort for my heart in special ways. I realized that as hard as I tried, I would never be able to be perfect in my own effort. I began to see my bitterness and was led to repentance of this. I needed His healing in my heart that allowed me to receive His extended forgiveness. This allowed me to extend it to others too. In this process, as I experienced healing, I wanted other people to also experience the love and grace of Jesus. He was so personal!

I began to use the same concept with the children in the classroom. When there was a wrongdoing committed, I would ask for wisdom to understand and care for the child's heart, desiring to help the child understand the love and comfort of Jesus. If their hearts opened to Him, it was not abnormal for them to receive peace from Him. This often resulted in a behavioral change. Sometimes it was a process and sometimes I saw changes overnight.

I'm so thankful for the love Jesus demonstrated by dying on the cross. This brought complete forgiveness for us! We don't need to work hard to earn that forgiveness. Because He rose from the dead, He showed the power He has over the enemy. He has power to break connections and lies that the enemy has planted in our minds through our damage. He longs to bring comfort, grace and healing to our damaged hearts. As we receive that compassion from Him, we will want others to experience His love also. The more I understand His grace toward me, the more I am able to grow in demonstrating the character of Jesus to others.

PRAYER:

Lord Jesus, it is so easy to see the faults of people around me. It's easy to focus on the wrongdoing in my own life. Is that what You focus on? Would You give me a picture of how You look at the faults in people? Do You care about the damage that my heart faces or has faced in the past? Is there any damage to my heart that You would like to bring to my attention today, Jesus? Would You show me what You do with children who have experienced that kind of hurt? Thank You for Your grace. Would You build grace into my life so I can offer it to those around me?

God's Grace
Demonstrated
to Our Hearts

Day 5

THE IMPORTANCE OF THE HEART

"Guard your heart above all else, for it determines the course of your life."
Proverbs 4:23

My heart...is it really so important? Why is it important? One day I asked the Lord, "Do YOU think my heart is important?"

His response to me was, "Your heart is like an engine in a car. The car cannot function without its engine. If the engine isn't taken care of, it won't run properly. It needs oil; it needs proper care and maintenance. So it is with your heart."

I was reminded of the verse, *"...What you say flows from what is in your heart."* Luke 6:45

Whatever my heart believes will determine my thoughts, and that will trigger my actions. When my heart feels like it is all bad, my thoughts about myself are negative, and I find myself taking unhealthy routes. I may try to prove to others or myself that I am acceptable. This results in trying hard to perform to make people around me happy. Then I can feel good about myself and counter all the badness--for a short time.

Other times I may believe that everything about myself is so negative that I hate myself. This produces a lack of motivation and purpose, and my mind can only focus on what I *wish* I could be. I have also compared myself with others whom I believed were not as good as me. This has led to thoughts of condemnation or judgment about people. In each of these scenarios my focus is on myself. It's like feeding my heart poison.

So what if I ask Jesus what He thinks about me? Who's right--Jesus or *me*? Whose belief system do I live by? If I hate myself, can I love others? If I speak negatively about myself, do others feel loved by me or do they feel pressured to convince me that I am of worth? When I put that pressure on them--silently or verbally--will they actually feel loved by me?

PRAYER:

Lord, what have I been believing about my heart? Have I been agreeing with You about it? Would You draw me a picture of what You see when <u>You</u> look at me? What words would You like to whisper into my heart right now, Lord? Have I been guarding my heart or have I been damaging it with my own words and thoughts about it? Have I been treating my heart like You would? Would You open the eyes of my heart in the coming days to see who You REALLY are and to see myself as YOU see me? I desire to agree with You about myself.

Day 6

FEELINGS - FRIEND OR FOE?

"The thief's purpose is to steal and kill and destroy. My purpose is to give them a rich and satisfying life." John 10:10

Emotions...what good are they? So many people are controlled by their emotions. People cry to get their way--even adults. People cry to manipulate and to get attention. People refuse to do things because they don't feel like it.

Let's look at the opposite. Some people don't or won't feel. Everything is done by what is logical. If they see a person hurting, their viewpoint and logic assesses the situation as to whether comfort is necessary. Many people have come into our office wishing for feeling from those closest to them. They long for understanding. It's easier to work hard, to serve, to minister, and to lead without feeling. If one doesn't have feeling, then they won't get hurt. People tend to run away from getting hurt. Why would that be?

The heart is the seat of feelings or emotion. All of what one does or thinks is a result of what is in his heart. It is quite natural for an individual to disregard his heart and to be logical about what seems right to him. In this method, most sensitivity is lost--and so is faith. Faith doesn't run along the same track as logic. Faith in God is following HIS track, not one's own.

For many years, I tried to do away with my sensitivity. It seemed to me that people looked down on it and I came to believe that I was too sensitive. As well, when my sensitivity did surface, I often became overwhelmed and felt like I was drowning in the sea of feelings. I only knew a few options: to live above them, ignore them or to be overwhelmed by them. The first option took much effort, pretending, and performance to prove to everyone I was okay. Ignoring them meant they didn't exist and I went into denial. The third option felt like I was living in a dark pit, shuffling through negativity and doom.

So what is God's intent for me? Is it possible that there is a different way to handle emotions? He gave me a heart. He made me in His image. He gave me feelings. He demonstrated sensitivity. Maybe emotions aren't so wrong after all! As I gave Jesus permission to pay attention to my hurting heart, I began to see His tenderness and compassion. I learned that having emotions was not sin. I responded to His invitation to look at my hurting, damaged heart. I experienced personal comfort from Him in ways I had never imagined possible. I began to get excited! I was not just excited about life, but excited about JESUS--the author of LIFE!

PRAYER:

Lord Jesus, You made me with a heart. Did You make my heart to feel? Have I been burying my feelings or running away from them? Have I been allowing my feelings to overwhelm me? Would You draw me a picture, give me a song, a verse or a Bible Story that would demonstrate why You gave me a heart to feel? What does it do to those around me when I live without feelings? What does it do to those around me when I am controlled by my feelings? Jesus, what would it look like if I let You pay attention to my heart? Would You open the ears of my heart to hear You?

Day 7

SELFISH OR NOT?

"...Love your neighbor as yourself." Matthew 22:39b

So often I hear the question, "Isn't it selfish to pay attention to my own heart?" In fact, I asked that very question myself at one time. What does Jesus mean when He said, "Love your neighbor as yourself"? I always was under the impression that the focus was on loving the neighbor. Yet, in the last number of years as my own heart has received more and more healing, I've understood that *my* heart also needs attention. That verse seems to assume that we should also love ourselves. Is it selfish to love? Love is of God; it is NOT selfishness.

God is love and Jesus came to show us the Father. Therefore, I believe it is important to agree with Jesus about who HE is, about who I am, as well as about others. How would Jesus treat my heart?

In my journey of learning the importance of my own heart, I've come to realize that when I disagree with Jesus' thoughts about me, I DO become selfish. Sometimes this is shown through defending myself to prove my point. When I've felt mistreated or misunderstood, I have criticized others with spoken or unspoken words. I have had self-pity when others said or insinuated unkind things. When this happens, my thoughts toward myself deteriorate, as does my love toward others.

Now that Jesus is becoming more personal to my heart, I often ask Him what He thinks. I like to come to Him as a little child (Mark 10:14-15). A child doesn't know all the answers and usually is eager to learn. A child's heart is open toward love. If I forget about coming as a child, my adult agenda and rationale can get in the way. As a little girl, I ask Him what He sees when He looks at me. I ask Him what He thinks of me. Sometimes I have a huge hurdle to jump. Will I believe what I think about myself, or will I agree with what He says about me? The more I understand who Jesus really is, the quicker my heart agrees with Him. Then I am able to love myself. Whatever is in my heart will spill out to those around me. If love is there, others will get the outpouring of Jesus' love without me trying hard to make it happen! In this way, I can love my neighbor as myself, and LOVE is NOT selfish!

PRAYER:

Lord Jesus, I am choosing to come to You as a child. There are so many things I don't know or understand about You and about me. Jesus, would You draw me a picture of what You think of me? How would you like to bring peace to my heart today? How have I been viewing my own heart? Have I been neglecting it, ignoring it, condemning it, or letting it do whatever it wants? Have I been in agreement with You, Jesus? What would You like to say to my heart today? I'd like to receive those things as a gift. Thank You, Jesus!

Day 8

THE ALARM SYSTEM

"The Lord is close to the brokenhearted; he rescues those whose spirits are crushed." Psalm. 34:18

My husband, Nevin, and his dad had just pulled out of the drive. I was going to be alone for the next week. "What if something happens to him?" "What if he never comes back?" "What if I'm left alone for the rest of my life?" The questions rolled into my head faster than I could speak them aloud.

What do we do with our feelings when they surface? This is an example of the feeling or emotion of fear. I could say to myself, "Joann, you are being ridiculous. Quit being afraid!" This would put me into the try-hard, performance way of dealing with this feeling. Ultimately, I would be stuffing the fear down inside to be "strong."

On the other hand, I could say to myself, "Joann, he may never come back! You are going to be all alone tonight and something bad might happen when he is away. What will you do if you are all by yourself?" I could allow the questions to multiply until the fear became very real and overwhelming. This is the way I had often done in the past.

This particular time I was able to let the feeling of fear be an alarm. An alarm is neither right nor wrong; it is just plain going off! My fear alarm was ringing pretty loud! So I started asking Jesus what He does with fearful girls. Within a few minutes, He brought peace with His promise to stay with me, to protect me, and to be with Nevin. Though He did not promise to keep both of us free from disappointment or casualty, He drew me a picture of His protection, promising that there would be abundant grace if I needed it.

Feelings will show up in many different forms: fear, negativity, criticism, frenzy, keeping busy and being unable to relax, anger, withdrawal, scorn, etc. The list goes on and on. Sometimes it takes those closest to me to let me know when I am reacting from feelings. Even if I think I'm not letting emotion control me, it often has a subtle way of taking over. We become familiar with our own reactions, having no idea how they may affect others. When I began to realize that my feelings were not sin, I was then able to start moving to the next step and ask, "Why do I feel this way?" or "From where does this come?"

When I define what is happening in my heart to set off the alarm, it is necessary to take my heart to Jesus for comfort. His compassion brings peace and then I am better able to accept the situation I'm experiencing. If I don't do this step, I am more likely to let fear, bitterness, blame, criticism, etc. grow.

That week while Nevin was gone, I was able to sleep each night. When thoughts of fear popped up, the picture Jesus had given me would often come into my mind. That picture gave me what I needed to rest in His comfort.

PRAYER:

Lord, today I invite You to prompt me when my heart is hurting. Would you help me know when the alarm is ringing? Did an alarm ring yesterday, Jesus? What did I do with that alarm? Teach me how to bring my heart to You when it is hurting so I don't need to take it out on myself or others. Would You draw me a picture of Your compassion?

Day 9

MY DAMAGED HEART

"The Spirit of the Lord is upon me, because he has anointed me to preach the gospel to the poor; He has sent me to heal the brokenhearted, to proclaim liberty to the captives and recovery of sight to the blind, to set at liberty those who are oppressed." Luke 4:18 (NKJV)

"How does my past affect what I do today?" "Why should I look at my past experiences? I've decided to not think about those things and move on!" These are comments that we hear as we interact with people.

What good does it do to look at my past hurts? When I was a child and very impressionable, is it possible that my heart developed a belief system about life and about myself from the things that happened to it? Is it possible that today's reactions come out of an unhealthy belief system that was built in my foundational years?

As I was growing up, I was very fearful. I became very familiar with the feeling of fear. I feared strange situations, I feared change, I feared the unknown, and many more things. I didn't know what to do with my fear. I would say, "That's just the way I am." Because of damage to my heart in various ways, I began to believe things about myself and God and about people that really were not true. Yet, I thought they were. Out of my belief system, I also passed on damage to other people.

I've heard people make the statement "That's just the way I am" about various things: anger, criticism, lacking motivation, impulsivity, perfectionism, depression, etc. Did God really make people fearful, critical, angry, unthinking, or perfectionistic? Could it be that we learned those ways of behavior from disappointment or damage in our past? The enemy desires to use our damage to build an unhealthy belief system. Our actions will come out of what we believe.

All of the above sounds like there is robbery going on. The enemy wants to rob us of the heart Jesus gave us so we don't enjoy life. Because we learn our belief system while young, our perception becomes truth to us.

All people are damaged because we live in a fallen world. We receive damage and we pass it on. Jesus came to heal the brokenhearted and to bind our wounds. He also came to forgive us of our sins, the negative reactions that come from our wounded hearts. By looking at our damage, and receiving the comfort of Jesus to our hearts, we are more able to forgive from the heart those who hurt us.

For me, that is becoming reality. As I allow Him to do healing in His way, He brings compassion and comfort to my heart. I am experiencing Him in more personal ways than I ever did before. My heart is also drawn toward Him rather than fearing consequences. My heart has been releasing those who hurt me, recognizing that they did it out of their own damage and hurt.

I have been learning that it is safe to admit my heart was damaged. My pain does not change who I am to Jesus. I am understanding some unhealthy messages that I believed from the past and these messages have affected how I relate to those around me. As I have allowed Jesus permission to move into the pain and put healing ointment on it, my heart is understanding in a whole new way who Jesus really is and who I am. My belief system is changing, as well as my responses to my sensitive triggers. Sometimes the changes are slow; sometimes they are faster. I am more clear on what is my responsibility and that I have the ability to make choices rather than fall into my "default" mode. This has been a whole new way of living for me. I am grateful for a patient and tender Jesus who has cared about my broken heart.

PRAYER:

Lord Jesus, what do You think of my heart? Would You like to bring understanding to me about the hurt that has been done to my heart? If I'm afraid to look at these things, what is causing my fear? What do You do with a child that is afraid, Jesus? Would You comfort my heart? Is there anything that You want to bring to my mind today that damaged my heart in the past? Lord, what did that damage do to my heart? Have I believed any messages or lies from that experience? What would You like to do with those lies? What would You like to put in their place? What would You like to do with my hurting heart, Jesus? Would You bring a picture of peace to my heart?

God's Grace Demonstrated Through His Character

Day 10

GOD, OUR ABBA FATHER

"Jesus said to him, "I am the way, the truth, and the life.
No one can come to the Father except through me.
If you had really known me,
you would know who my Father is.
From now on, you do know him and have seen him!"
John 14:6-7

"Anyone who has seen me has seen the Father!" John 14:9

"I have loved you even as the Father has loved me. Remain in my love."
John 15:9

Is it okay to talk to Jesus in a way that brings Him to our level? This is a question that we occasionally hear from people. I know a father who has young children. He loves spending time with his children. It is not uncommon to see him on the floor interacting with them. This does not change who he is; he is still the father. Yet he is willing to get on their level and relate to them right where they are.

Our God is holy. He is mighty, omniscient, and worthy of our worship and praise. There is no doubt about that. That is Who He is! This same God sent His Son to walk the earth with mankind. Jesus lived life as we do. He knows the difficulty of living on this earth. He knows how to relate to us on our level. He saw short Zaccheus up in the tree and went to his home. He visited his friends Mary, Martha, and Lazarus in their home. There are many accounts of how Jesus related to people as He walked on earth as a human.

In John 14 Jesus tells his disciples that anyone who has seen Him has seen the Father. When Jesus came to earth, He was a physical snapshot of God the Father. Jesus was the Shepherd, a Friend, the Healer, and much more. Jesus interacted personally with the people around Him. Jesus also said that when He left, He would send the Comforter in the person of the Holy Spirit. His presence would continue to be available. Galatians 4:6-7 says, *"And because we are his children, God has sent the Spirit of his Son into our hearts, prompting us to call out, 'Abba, Father.' Now you are no longer a slave but God's own child. And since you are his child, God has made you his heir."*

Is it not exciting that God our Father sees us as His children? As our Abba Father, He understands our immaturity. He speaks our language. He knows our hurts. He knows our potential. His love for us is so intense that we cannot begin to understand the extent of it. Just as an earthly father wants to be a safe place for his children to process life with him, so God our Father longs to have us process all of life with Him. As we are able to receive this love that He has for us, His love has power to influence us to become more like Him.

We will never be motivated to become like someone of whom we are afraid. The enemy would like us to believe that God is harsh, forceful and too rigid for us. The enemy wants to distort the character of God so that we won't be drawn to Him as a Father. By believing these things, we give the enemy the upper hand in our lives. His tactic is to attack God's people and try to control us and our thinking. The enemy can only get back at God by convincing us that his lies are truth. This gives him power over us and draws us away from the loving, personal Father God. If we have a warped view of who God is, we will remain distanced from Him believing He is against us.

How thankful we can be that our Abba Father continues to pursue us even when we struggle to trust Him because of the bad things that happen to us! How thankful we can be that He never changes and that He will forever be a loving, Abba Father!

PRAYER:

Lord, thank You for allowing me to be Your child. Thank you for providing a way back to You so I don't have to live in the separation that sin brought into the world. Today, Lord, I would like my heart to understand more about You. Are there any lies that I have been believing about You? When did my heart start believing those lies? Would You disconnect that lie from my heart and show me truth about You? Will You put into my mind a thought, song, picture, story, or something that helps my heart grasp more of Your character? How would You like to show me what You think of me? Thank You for Your love and thank You that You are my loving Father!

Day 11

IS GOD GOOD?

"The thief's purpose is to steal and kill and destroy. My purpose is to give them a rich and satisfying life. I am the good shepherd..." John 10:10-11

"Whatever is good and perfect is a gift coming down to us from God our Father, who created all the lights in the heavens. He never changes or casts a shifting shadow." James 1:17

When God created mankind, He gave the gift of choice to all. When Adam and Eve took of the fruit, sin came into the world. Now all people are born with a sin nature. Thankfully, because of God's intense love for us, He provided a way back to Himself. The enemy, who is out to steal, kill, and destroy, wants to rob us of our relationship with a loving God. He tries to use the bad things in life to convince us that we have little choice and that we are victims of our circumstances. When we believe that we have no choice in difficulties, we feel helpless and allow ourselves to be controlled. We open ourselves up to the possibility of allowing the negative circumstances or difficulties to affect our thinking about God's goodness. This is one form of the enemy's robbery.

Through Jesus, God showed us a representation of Himself. God is love, and because Jesus came, He offered abundant life to us! Sometimes we may wonder how we can have abundant life in the midst of bad or difficult circumstances. If our belief system has been warped by our damage, we will often begin to question God's love toward us. We want to be rescued from the bad things. When we are not rescued, the enemy tries to attack our belief system in an attempt to distort who God really is. This way God gets the blame for bad things that happen instead of the enemy.

The younger we are when trauma happens in our life, the more probable it is that our belief system about God will be warped. Our warped perception from our traumatic experiences become "truth" to us. In this way doubt about the goodness of God develops. This keeps us from being drawn to Him. This also will hinder our ability to hear from Him.

It may be necessary at times to focus on the FACT of who God is. One way of doing this is to write down the things God shows us about Himself or the ways that He ministers to our hearts. In times of doubt, we can go back and be reminded of how He has worked. We may wish to read Scriptures that focus on how Jesus interacted with people in their hurts. This may help our hearts focus on the truth of who He is as shown in Ps. 86:15. *"But you, O Lord are a God of compassion and mercy, slow to get angry and filled with unfailing love and faithfulness."*

PRAYER:

Lord, there have been times that I have doubted Your goodness. Is there a significant event that has happened to me in the past that has caused me to doubt You? Where were You, Lord, when that happened? What were You doing? Why didn't You rescue me? What do You do with doubting children? Is there a way You could restore security and trust to my heart again? Thank You for being my Shepherd. What one thing would You like to show my heart today?

Day 12

GOD'S GIFT OF GRACE

"Trust in the Lord with all your heart; do not depend on your own understanding." Proverbs 3:5

"So let us come boldly to the throne of our gracious God. There we will receive his mercy, and we will find grace to help us when we need it most." Hebrews 4:16

Grace. In Greek this word means "favor or kindness." This favor is free. What does this word mean for me personally?

I invested so much effort in my life trying to do what I should. There were expectations from family, friends, the church, myself and even from God. I tried hard to make them all happy. When I fell short, I knew I was a failure. It was all my fault. These continual screw-ups made for a depressive life. My try-hard mentality actually became a way of depending on myself to become a person of integrity.

In talking with others, some can't identify with my past approach to life. They know they can achieve. They have learned how to measure up to the expectation "bar" that has been held over them. In asking the question, "What would happen if you don't reach the bar?" these people have responded, "I have to make it." These people also depend on their own abilities to measure up to the standard.

Is it possible that I have come to depend upon myself to live right? It is easy to get trapped into the idea that how I perform will change the way Jesus thinks about me. I focus on my performance or lack of it. Out of this mentality, I can put pressure on others to perform to my standards or I put pressure on myself to perform to their standards.

Jesus invites us to shift our focus. He went to the cross. He shed His blood. He rose again, and because of this, He gives life; He gives *grace*! I like to envision Him standing at the door of His infinite warehouse of grace. As He looks at me, He calls me to receive the gift of grace. When I intentionally or unintentionally fall, He reaches His hand to me and extends me His gift--grace! I may stand there with my eyes cast down and try to convince Him that I am undeserving. What He wants most is for me to meet His eye and reach out to accept the gift of grace that He is extending. As I reach for the gift, my eyes lift to meet His tender, compassionate, approving gaze. It is really about Him. My identity is really about what He thinks, His understanding of me! The more I experience His grace, the more I will be drawn to Him and His character.

One day I asked Jesus for a picture of His grace. The picture He brought was of the waves coming in on the edge of a seashore or ocean. Over and over the waves come in. That picture of grace brings my heart comfort. It is always there!

Each day I have a choice. I will fall at times. That is not failure. The question is, "What will I do when I fall? Will I look up into the face of a tenderhearted Jesus and reach out to His extended hand of grace?"

PRAYER:

Lord, I don't think I understand a lot about Your grace. Would You draw a picture of Your grace for me? Are there ways that I have been trusting in my own understanding instead of accepting Your understanding of me? Jesus, would You show me on what I have been focusing? I don't think I know how to keep my focus on You. Would You give me just one thing to think about today?

Day 13

GOD'S FAITHFULNESS DURING RAIN OR SHINE

"Great is his faithfulness; his mercies begin afresh each morning."
Lamentations 3:23

"As long as the earth remains, there will be planting and harvest, cold and heat, summer and winter, day and night." Genesis 8:22

"He covers the heavens with clouds, provides rain for the earth, and makes the grass grow in mountain pastures." Psalm 147:8

Rain! Uggghhh! I dislike it very much. I'll tell you why…things get soooo wet! If there is too much rain, the ground gets muddy. I can't work outside, and it ruins plans like camping, outdoor activities and other things. It keeps children inside and they don't get fresh air. Everything just gets soaked and it is not pleasant. I go to sit on my outside bench and get all wet. The overcast skies make it seem dark and dreary. It gets depressing. I think I'd do just fine without rain, or would I?

I like the sun! Day after day the brightness from the sun lifts my spirits. When the sun shines, it is so nice to be outside and enjoy the fresh air. Plans don't get ruined as quickly due to weather. There's warmth. I like it when everything isn't soggy outside and I can enjoy the flowers and the rest of God's creation. I love sitting on my swing and talking to Jesus in the sunlight! The sun reminds me of His love for me. Keep the sun coming!

That was all before I experienced summertime in Kansas! There are many days of sunlight. Not just a little sunlight, but lots of it! One summer the triple digits brought an over-abundance of warmth and it became very dry. Daily we needed to water the garden, the flowers, and the grass. When we left for trips, we needed to find someone to water for us. And even with all the watering, the garden didn't produce like we had hoped that year. Some of the flowers shriveled up because the heat was so hard on them. My lovely mother's day hanging basket became nothing. I was so disappointed. Our weekend of camping was shortened due to the heat. The sun was just too intense at 10:00 in the morning! Bike rides were not a thought. Playing outdoor recreational games wasn't even alluring. The crops of our farmer friends became a concern and everywhere we went, we heard talk about the weather...I mean serious talk.

I realized how much my personal life can be like that. I want the good days, the sunny days, the warmth of relationships. It's easier to see God's faithfulness when I'm in a good mood. I think I can do without the difficult, messy days--the rain. They can be so hard. I can lose focus of what God is doing. Yet, when there is only sun, things become dried up. My heart begins to wither.

I need both. I need the sun and the rain. I'm glad that in God's faithfulness to me, He knows what I need. If all things are easy in life, growth won't happen. Strength comes from learning to combat the difficult things. I am drawn to call on God in those difficult times. The rain keeps the new growth from becoming wilted. It builds stamina. The sun brings warmth; it brings refreshment after the rain. I see the beauty during the sunshine, but it comes because of the rain. I guess God knows what He's doing to bring the rain and the sun!

PRAYER:

Thank You, Lord, for Your faithfulness in the midst of the sun and the rain. What kind of season is my heart in? Is it

drying up and wilting? What is causing that? Is my heart discouraged from all the chaos going on around me? How would You like to speak to my heart today? Have I become so focused on what I want that I don't see the gifts You bring with the rain? Lord, what would You like to show me about Yourself today?

God's Grace Demonstrated Through Communication

Day 14

FEAR OR LOVE?

"...Anyone who has seen me has seen the Father!..." John 14:9

"I have loved you even as the Father has loved me. Remain in my love."
John 15:9

"Perfect love casts out fear..." I John 4:18

I remember as a child hearing a sermon about hell. I didn't want to go to hell and decided I better ask Jesus into my heart so I wouldn't go there. For many years I tried hard to do the right things to make sure He approved of me so I could go to Heaven. This way of living eventually became very draining to me and sure did not bring me much security.

My fear has been one area that has hindered me in hearing from Jesus. My whole salvation experience was based on fear of what He would do to me if I did wrong. My fear of His disapproval did not make Him a safe place for me to pour out my heart. Yet I knew I should want to go to Him and felt guilty because I wasn't drawn to Him. The "Jesus" I knew was not very inviting!

So is Jesus someone to be feared? In John 14:9 Jesus told His disciples that when they had seen Him, they had seen the Father. John also says that God is love. That would indicate that Jesus is love also! When someone truly loves us, will they pressure us to be what they want through disapproval, high expectations, condemnation, etc.? Jesus didn't do this when He was on earth and still doesn't. It has been a steep learning curve for my heart to learn who Jesus really is...and I'm still on that journey.

I have often been asked, "How can my view of Jesus change?" In my experience, this did not happen overnight. I began reading simple Bible stories to myself and talking to my heart about who Jesus is. I read through the book of John and meditated on how Jesus related to the common people, such as the disciples, the woman at the well, the sick, etc. When I would come up against difficult situations in life, I would ask myself how Jesus would respond to those people. This process took time. In this way, when I would converse with Him, I would visualize myself talking with the Jesus I was reading about in the Bible stories. This Jesus began to draw me to Himself and I wanted to learn more about Him.

Others have been drawn to Him through their God-given gifts of art and music, as well as through nature. There are numerous creative ways that can lead us to discovering more about Jesus. We can ask Him how He wants to open that door. God is capable of changing our belief systems if we are open to change. *"...And the Lord--who is the Spirit--makes us more and more like him as we are changed into his glorious image." 2 Corinthians 3:18*

PRAYER:

Lord Jesus, my view of You has been warped. I find myself afraid of Your disapproval, Your condemnation or Your correction. In that fear, I am not drawn to You. What has caused me to be afraid of You? When did that fear begin? Would You draw me a picture that would describe my belief about You now? In the coming hours, days, and weeks would You show me who You really are? Would You put an idea in my mind that would help me develop truth about You? What is one thing, Lord, that You would like me to know about You today?

Day 15

I CAN'T SEEM TO HEAR HIM

"When they call on me, I will answer; I will be with them in trouble. I will rescue and honor them." Psalm 91:15

In my journey of developing a personal relationship with Jesus there have been many times that I could hear nothing from Him. In fact, when I first began talking to Him in a personal way, I often didn't hear Him. I would get very frustrated and blame myself for not knowing how to do it right. At times I would be convinced that He didn't want to talk with me. This frustration made me want to quit. I'm glad I didn't, but learning to hear His voice has been a process.

What has kept me from hearing the voice of my Shepherd? Many times I was afraid that He wouldn't speak or that He would say something I didn't want to hear. I feared His correction or punishment. Sometimes I had my own agenda. Sometimes I was not in a mood to hear anything and I was conversing with Him because I needed to do the right thing. Sometimes my heart was so focused on all the negative circumstances going on around me, I didn't believe He would help in the seemingly impossible situations. Other times I wanted only what He would do for me. Sometimes He spoke, but I didn't recognize Him. This list is not exhaustive.

I am learning to approach Him as a child with an open heart who does not know all the answers (Mark 10:14-15). When I come in this way, I can say whatever I want to say without pressure to do it the right way. I often envision Him sitting in a chair close to me or holding me. If I am anxious, I ask Him what is causing that fear. A friend once encouraged me to write down the first thoughts that come to my mind whether or not they make sense to me. As long as these thoughts do not contradict Scripture, my part is to walk in faith that these are words from Him. This has been helpful. When I ask Him a question, I just wait to hear from Him. Through these times of conversing with Jesus, I have come to know Him in a much deeper way.

There are times when I talk to Jesus that I hear nothing. Instead of allowing my anxiety to rise thinking that He doesn't care or that I am doing something wrong, I'm learning to relax. I often ask Him if something is standing in the way of hearing Him. If a word comes to mind, I will resist the enemy or repent of that thing. Otherwise, I think about some of the last things I heard from Him. I tell Him that I will hold onto the previous words until He wants to say something else. This requires faith and is not always easy.

My journey to hear Jesus continues. If I focus on the *hearing* part, I get frustrated. If I focus on my *relationship* with Him, I remember He is my friend, my Father, my Savior, and my Healer. I also am more likely to remember that I am His child and that He delights in me. This opens my heart to hear Him and has drawn me to anticipate spending more time with Him.

PRAYER:

Jesus, my heart isn't used to talking with You on a personal level. I'm afraid You won't talk to me. I'm afraid I won't hear You. Would You draw me a picture of what You do with fearful children? Jesus, are You distant? Would You show me where You are right now? Where am I in that picture, Lord? Is there a song that You'd like to put in my heart that would tell me a little bit about who You are? Where are You when it seems so quiet? Is there anything in my life that is blocking me from hearing You? What do You think when Your children want to sit down with You and chat? Jesus, what would You like to talk about now? Thank You for spending time with me.

Day 16

I DON'T FEEL ANY DIFFERENT

"Don't copy the behavior and customs of this world, but let God transform you into a new person by changing the way you think..." Romans 12:2

"Faith is the confidence that what we hope for will actually happen; it gives us assurance about things we cannot see." Hebrews 11:1

Winter in the north brought about some very cold days. Sometimes snow activities lured us outside into subzero weather. Somehow that cold air managed to attack the body's extremities by seeping inside any heavy clothing. Upon returning to the warm house, the numb, stiff fingers and toes stung as they began to thaw. The warmth did not immediately remove the stiffness; it was a process of time. What a relief, though, when feeling and mobility returned!

Sometimes a numb heart is the same way. When we have spent years of putting our feelings aside, they will not immediately start showing themselves. It's always nice to have the warm, fuzzy feelings that *seem* to be a part of "everybody else's" lives.

Sometimes in prayer Jesus will show us pictures or say specific words to us. There are times we do not feel any different inside. The enemy can use this void to convince us that nothing is going to change. We tend to want immediate results. At these times it may be necessary to walk in faith, thanking Him for the truths He has shown us. We may need to focus on the FACT rather than the feeling. We can tell Him that we would enjoy experiencing the results, but invite Him to bring those feelings in His time.

The transformation process is often not instant. In fact it may feel at times like things get worse for awhile--just like the stinging of frozen fingers when they are thawing. It takes faith, courage, and perseverance. With faith we cannot always see results, but we have hope in the person of Jesus. We may fear that nothing will change, but courage helps us continue. The inability to feel different can entice us to give up. Perseverance will keep our focus on Jesus, knowing that this life is really about Him and not us!

PRAYER:

Lord, it's hard to keep talking to You when I don't feel any different inside. It's a whole lot easier to tell You all my needs or express the needs of others. It's easier to make our time a time of business--I tell you what I need and then You are expected to supply it. But to stay and chat...to wait...to listen...to converse back...Lord, that is a whole different story. When You show me things that seem like truth and I don't feel different inside, it is easy to doubt what You said and question myself. What would courage look like? In the days to come, would You bring feelings into my heart? How would You like to build perseverance into this journey? I can't do this by myself. Thank You for being my strength.

Day 17

DUTY OR RELATIONSHIP?

"...Come to me, all of you who are weary and carry heavy burdens, and I will give you rest." Matthew 11:28-30

"God sent his Son into the world not to judge the world, but to save the world through him." John 3:17

"I know I need to spend time with God, but it is such a struggle!" These are words I've heard over and over. It seems it is a common struggle. What would cause this?

Why do we feel pressured to have "time with God"? Is it because it is an expected Christian duty? Have we been using this discipline to measure our spirituality? There are continual reminders about reading, meditating and memorizing Scripture. These are all definitely important. Does God desire that we focus on these disciplines or on Himself?

There is often pressure from the Christian community to do the right things in the right ways. For the person who is sensitive to pressure, this can lead to comparison and can become a measuring stick for spirituality. The focus can begin to shift from a relationship with a personal Jesus to obedience or performance for Him. Were we intended to be human *beings* or human *doings*?

What would it look like if our focus is on Jesus? When I was dating Nevin, we enjoyed hanging out together. We enjoyed travelling together and doing a variety of things together. We were motivated to learn more about each other and anticipated our times together. It was a mutual experience. The more I learned to know this man, the more I liked the idea of spending my life with him.

So it is with Jesus. He doesn't desire that it be about duty. He longs for a personal relationship with us. He longs to just spend time with us. He created us, giving us a heart and gifts that make us unique. He delights to see us experience living out of that heart! He longs to have us receive His gifts and enjoy them. Who better understands our hearts than our Creator?!

The more we understand who Jesus is and His heart for us, the more we will be drawn to Him. He was not sent to condemn us, but to demonstrate a picture of love!

In my personal life, my relationship with Jesus is becoming more of a lifestyle rather than an appointment that I need to keep with Him each morning. I enjoy personal times set aside to talk with Him. Sometimes He speaks to me from His Word. Sometimes He helps me sort out priorities for my day. Sometimes He will say what He thinks of me and often will show Himself to me in personal ways. He removes emotional pressure and helps me manage the daily pressures. He invites me into deeper relationship with Him.

PRAYER:

Lord, sometimes I find myself coming to You out of duty. I find myself measuring my spirituality by doing the right disciplines. Sometimes I find myself coming to You for what You can do for me. Then I'm disillusioned when it doesn't happen the way I had hoped. Jesus, what would a personal relationship with You look like? How would that be different than it is now? Jesus, do you enjoy spending time with me? Is there a song we could sing together? What song would that be? Would You enjoy walking through this day with me? What is one thing You would like to invite me into today?

God's Grace Demonstrated in the Daily Grind

Day 18

THE TWO DITCHES

"Unfailing love and truth have met together. Righteousness and peace have kissed!" Psalms 85:10

"...we will speak the truth in love, growing in every way more and more like Christ, who is the head of his body, the church." Ephesians 4:15

We recently made the trip from Kansas to Minnesota. We travelled on the road and had smooth driving and a very good trip. What if we had taken the ditch? There would have been quite a few obstacles to avoid and I am quite certain we would not have reached our destination without many an incident.

Most of my life I lived in one ditch. I had a strong sense of right and wrong. It was important to do things right or there would be punishment. It was important to do things right to make people happy. It was important to do things right to keep Jesus happy. I worked very hard to do the right things. Being imperfect, I didn't always do right, but I tried very hard. This became even more important as I became an adult. The desire to do right grew and my effort increased.

This try-hard mentality seems to run rampant among people. It doesn't leave room for failure. If failure happens, we must make sure we correct it. We berate ourselves. If other people fail, often we will criticize them believing they should know better. I liken this mentality to one ditch. It is the ditch of truth, of right living, of performing right. We try so hard to be a good person. Often in this ditch we don't leave room for failure. Failure is the enemy. If we fail, we must quickly correct it. This method really puts the effort on myself to be successful. It expresses itself in these types of comments, "I must be a good Christian," "I must be a good teacher," "I must be a good parent," "I must do life well," etc. The pressure is on. It's all up to *me*.

There is another ditch. It is no safer than the other. This is the ditch of "love" and "grace". This ditch says we can do what we want because God forgives. We may hear comments like, "I'm a believer so it doesn't matter what I do," or " I can do what I feel like because Jesus loves me." Or we may hear, "I'm free in Christ and He forgives; I'm not bound by legalism!" This mentality is also about doing what *I* want.

It doesn't seem to matter which ditch we are in, we certainly don't want to fall into the opposite one! In fact, if we listen to ourselves, we may find ourselves judging those who are in the opposite ditch. This keeps us stuck in the one with which we are familiar. Sometimes we become bitter because we were raised in one ditch or the other. Avoiding that ditch becomes our focus. In our intensity against it, we fall into the other ditch and begin to judge those who hurt us.

What would it mean to live on the "road?" As I accept Jesus' hand of grace, I will leave the ditch of performance. As I accept His grace and understand His value for me, I won't need to perform perfectly to gain acceptance. The more grace I receive from Him, the more I will see that I need Him in every part of my life. I will be drawn to a Jesus of love and be motivated to live in a way that demonstrates His character. My desire for righteous living will not be out of obligation but a result of love and a relationship *with* Jesus.

What would happen in my daily life if my focus was on a relationship *with* Jesus instead of working *for* Him or receiving *from* Him? If my focus is on relationship with Him and I desire to learn about His character, will I do just what *I* want? On the other hand, if I have a relationship with Jesus, will I have to be perfect and right to be acceptable to Him? Will there be room for grace for myself? He is extending it!

PRAYER:

Lord Jesus, have I fallen into a ditch? If so, which one am I in? Am I in the one that I feel like I can do whatever I want or the ditch of performing right to be acceptable? Would You show my heart what You think of me? Have I been accepting Your thoughts of me? Have I been trying hard to live *for* You? Have I been interested only in what I can receive *from* You? Lord, what would being in relationship *with* You look like today?

Day 19

WHOSE YOKE ARE YOU WEARING?

"...Come to me, all of you who are weary and carry heavy burdens, and I will give you rest. Take my yoke upon you. Let me teach you, because I am humble and gentle at heart, and you will find rest for your souls. For my yoke is easy to bear, and the burden I give you is light."
Matthew 11:28-30

I sat down one morning completely overwhelmed. There was so much to do and so little time to do it. I decided to take time and just talk to Jesus about the day. It seemed that it was going to be an impossible one! As I told Him my thoughts, He gave me the idea to write everything down that was important for that day. I did this and the list was lengthy. I told Him I'd like to carry *His* yoke for the day instead of *mine*. With this in mind, I asked what was important to Him. My mind was drawn to one thing on the list. I agreed that would be a good place to start. Wanting to be efficient, I asked Him what He wanted me to do after that. His answer was a bit surprising. He told me I could come back when the first thing was done and then ask Him what should be next. I decided to take Him up on that offer. That day I did not get everything completed on my list, yet I had such a feeling of accomplishment. He allowed me time to rest as well as time to work, and I was also able to keep Him in focus throughout my day. He gave rest to my overwhelmed state.

Whenever I take the time to talk with Jesus about my day and willingly give up my agenda, I can actually be motivated to do the mundane things. It's not abnormal for me to **know** what needs to be accomplished in a day. Often the thought to let Him show me what is most important doesn't even surface to my mind. Unfortunately, this causes me to forget that I need my Teacher, the one who gives rest. When I plan my days, it is so easy to put pressure on my heart to be productive. My focus is on what I should be doing or on what I think is important. I tend to lose sight of His invitation to take on *His* yoke.

I have found this to be one of the most practical ways to care for my heart. I can't care for my heart without Him. My own ideas and agenda take over. Whenever I try to care for my heart by myself, I will most often end up in self-focus. This will cause me to put pressure on myself or on those close to me. It will often lead me to defend myself if I feel like I'm being misunderstood. When I involve Jesus in caring for my heart, it gets the best care possible. A loving Teacher is there to gently guide me in the process of living life.

PRAYER:

Lord Jesus, there is so much around me that needs attention. When I think of all that seems important, I can get so discouraged. You've told me I can find rest if I come to You and take Your yoke. Jesus, would You draw a picture for me of what that would look like? Is there someone in Scripture that You would like to bring to mind who took Your yoke? When I do what is reasonable to me, others around me can feel pressure. It also puts pressure on myself. Is there a different way? Would You show me what is important for me right now? Is there a word or a song that You would like me to focus on today? I don't understand true rest. Throughout the day, would You show me Your rest? Thank you for being my gentle Teacher!

Day 20

THEY DON'T UNDERSTAND!

"O Lord, you have examined my heart and know everything about me.
You know when I sit down or stand up. You know my thoughts even
when I'm far away." Psalm 139:1-2

One morning Nevin and I were having a normal conversation. I had a question about where a certain building was in town and proceeded to say where I thought it was. Confused with my description, he attempted to show me in his way where it was located. He said the same thing I did, only using his own words and description. I immediately assumed he was just trying to correct my way of describing it. Our perfectly "normal" conversation had turned sour. I became defensive because I felt invalidated and it seemed he was trying to tell me I was wrong. He had stepped on one of my triggers and I felt misunderstood. An insignificant subject suddenly became very significant. Thankfully we caught on to what was happening and were able to talk about the misunderstanding.

There will always be potential of being misunderstood in a relationship. When I'm feeling misunderstood, it is so easy to think only about the message that I want the other person to hear. My focus can so subtly shift from a healthy conversation to a demand that they understand me. I may begin to raise my voice, or I may withdraw and not talk or have some other reaction. These approaches do not enhance the relationship.

We all have a desire to be understood. Sometimes the people around us are interested in our thoughts and sometimes they really don't seem to be. They know they are right and there is no reason for more conversation. What can I do when I'm left feeling unheard and misunderstood? What does my heart need?

Sometimes I've found it is important to get alone to discuss the situation with Jesus. I ask Him if He understands what my heart is wanting. I often ask Him to draw me a picture that shows my hurting heart and how He wants to bring assurance to it. As I begin calming down on the inside, I ask Him what happened to raise my frustration level. Why did I *need* to be understood by the individual? Everyone longs for acceptance and sometimes I believe my acceptance comes only if people understand me. As I talk with Jesus and become reassured of His acceptance, He invites me to release the person who couldn't seem to understand. He will often ask me if His understanding of my heart is enough. Sometimes it takes some wrestling to release that desire to Him and accept His understanding as enough. When I do, I am able to experience peace more quickly and focus once again on the relationship. The longer I stay in the mode that demands understanding from the other person, the less likely I am to accept Jesus' understanding of me.

PRAYER:

Lord, I'm feeling so misunderstood and unheard by _____. I want to be heard. Jesus, do You see my heart? He/she doesn't seem to think my thoughts are valid. What do You think? Why do I get defensive when I'm misunderstood? Is that connected to something from my past? How would You like to bring comfort to my heart? Is my heart ready to release him/her from understanding me? When I demand that he/she understands, what does that do to his/her heart? Thank You, Jesus, for understanding me and knowing my thoughts!

Day 21

THE TREASURE HUNT

"For the love of Christ controls and urges and impels us,...."
I Corinthians 5:14a (AMP)

"Yet amid all these things we are more than conquerors and gain a surpassing victory through Him Who loved us." Romans 8:37 (AMP)

A few years ago Nevin spent many working hours putting raised beds in our garden. Our heavy, clay soil made it difficult to till, water properly, and drain excess water. Our choices boiled down to the following: 1. Have no garden and leave it as grass, 2. Leave the soil as it was and have a half-hearted crop, or 3. Change the soil, enrich it, work on the Bermuda grass that wanted to intrude, and put in raised beds. The latter meant a lot of hard work, but hopefully a much better garden.

Change can be hard work, especially when it comes to personal issues. Looking honestly at what is happening inside can be risky. We may find it hard to talk about personal things and find ourselves withdrawing or detaching. We may find it difficult to keep from going to anger or getting defensive in times that are overwhelming. We may find ourselves being "driven." These methods close our hearts to relationship. We find it much easier to continue in our familiar patterns, but they do not bring us or those around us "life." We don't like it when other people use these unhealthy patterns, but we may justify why we do them. We may find ourselves judging others and placing "shoulds" or expectations on them. But what about us? What keeps us from changing?

One of the first steps toward changing is admitting that there is a problem. Upon this admission we may even seek help to change the problem. Yet, as we live life, we find ourselves going back to the old, familiar ways and becoming discouraged. We wonder what we can do to make change happen faster.

In my journey of recognizing that I had some unhealthy patterns that needed to be changed, I was one of those who became discouraged with the slow process. I used to get impatient with myself that I couldn't get it right. This didn't help at all. As time went on, I started using a different approach. I try to use these times as opportunities for a "treasure hunt." When I recognize an unhealthy response in my life, I like to ask Jesus what prompted it. Instead of getting discouraged at myself, I try to use it as an opportunity to see what Jesus wants to tell me about my heart. These times of talking with Jesus have helped me learn more about myself. When I'm convicted about a time that I got angry, I ask Him what was happening in my heart to provoke the anger. I ask Him if my heart was longing for something. I then ask Him when I first felt that way and what He would like to do with my hurting heart. When I opt to bring my heart to Jesus, I don't get so overwhelmed with all the things that need to be changed. I also find out more about who Jesus is.

When Nevin worked on making our raised beds, they didn't happen overnight. It took shovelful after shovelful of new dirt. He kept plugging away on it until eventually we had a new garden. Because the soil had been changed, our crops grew much better. This is the way it is with the garden of our hearts. Each time we bring them to Jesus for more healing, for comfort, or for teaching from Him, the better the "soil" becomes. We learn a little bit more about who He is and His intense love for us. As we personally experience His love, we are drawn to obey Him. If our focus is on Him rather than on changing ourselves, we will become more like Him.

PRAYER:

Lord, I keep trying to change, but I get so discouraged. It seems nothing is happening very fast and I keep doing the same things over and over. I keep hurting the people I love most. Jesus, why do I keep _____? When did I start reacting that way? How was my heart hurt? Did I find this reaction modeled in my home? Was it an acceptable way of relating? Jesus, would You draw me a picture of how You would like to disconnect this from my heart? What messages did I learn about myself when I was young? About others? What truths would You like to plant into my heart instead, Lord? What would You like to do with my discouragement? What would You like to show me about Your love for me personally? Renew my vision, Lord!

Day 22

WHO'S THE CARETAKER OF YOUR ORCHARD?

"I am the true grapevine, and my Father is the gardener. He cuts off every branch of mine that doesn't produce fruit, and he prunes the branches that do bear fruit so they will produce even more...Those who remain in me, and I in them, will produce much fruit. For apart from me you can do nothing." John 15:1, 2, 4

One warm spring day I wandered out to our orchard. Perusing the barren peach trees, I wondered, "What will the coming months bring?" Since it was early in the season, I knew that frost could still prevent any fruit. There could also be hail, bugs, rust, etc. There were no guarantees. We could only wait and hope. We did get some fruit that year, but there were some things that had to be done to contribute to the possibility of fruit.

Throughout the winter when it all looked unproductive, Nevin would occasionally water the trees. Before there were buds, he pruned out some of their branches. I thought maybe he took too many off by the looks of the limbs laying on the ground. When the fruit was small, he did an even more "awful" thing. He wanted me to help in this process! We had to take off about 2/3 of the fruit on the loaded trees! I tried to close my eyes as I saw him "haphazardly" plucking off the fruit. I was sure he was going way overboard. He thought I was a bit frugal in my plucking. As the caretaker of the orchard, he knew what would give the tree full potential to make bigger and better fruit. In my lack of expertise, all I could think of was the amount of fruit being removed.

Weeks later, as the peaches developed and hung low, we put ropes around the trees so the fruit wouldn't distort and destroy branches. This didn't look very nice to the eye. Then we waited for the ripening...

Sometimes that is the way I have been in my emotional healing journey. I know the fruit I want, and I want it NOW! I try to rush the process. I get tired of the waiting game and have given up at times when I couldn't see results fast enough. If Nevin had forgotten about those trees in the winter because they looked so worthless, if he had not prepared the soil before planting them, or had not pruned consistently or thinned them, the potential for fruit would have been minimal. Some of those things he did years earlier hoping to someday see fruit.

To make good fruit within myself is impossible. It is God who gives the fruit. My job is to be a "servant" to my heart. I can make sure it has proper nutrients, make sure it is watered, and allow the Caregiver to prune and thin it without resistance, etc. My job isn't to decide **when** the fruit comes or to create the size of it. I do need to allow my heart to be an available place to grow fruit.

In the process of growing the peaches, my focus had been on the peaches (the fruit). Nevin, the caregiver, had his focus on the maintenance process. He recognized his limitations of producing fruit, but also recognized how he could contribute towards providing healthy conditions for the fruit. Neither of us could control the wind or hail or other hardships that our peaches have endured. It's amazing to see how they cling to their vine in their vulnerability.

Due to Nevin's faithful maintenance, our trees have potential to produce peaches if the outside conditions allow it. The fruit we have received has been a gift and we enjoy sharing it with others. Though the process of taking our hearts to Jesus for continued nurture can seem difficult and unending, the gift of fruit that He brings makes the journey worthwhile. This is the fruit that the people around us get to "eat."

PRAYER:

Lord, sometimes I get impatient. I find myself not trusting You in the process of growing. I want instant results and I don't like the difficult things that come into my life. Why do I get so impatient? Are there things that You would like to prune out of my life that I am resisting? Have I have been telling You how You should take care of me? If so, why do I do this? How would You bring encouragement to my heart today? What do I need to know about You? About myself? About others around me?

Day 23

RECEIVING AND GIVING LOVE

"We love each other because he loved us first." I John 4:19

"This is how much God loved the world: He gave his Son, his one and only Son. And this is why: so that no one need be destroyed; by believing in him, anyone can have a whole and lasting life." John 3:16 (MSG)

What do you do when you are given a compliment? Is it easy for you to receive it, or do you need to say something negative about yourself or quickly return a compliment? What about receiving an unexpected gift from somebody? Can you receive it and enjoy it or do you need to rationalize within yourself why they would give you that gift? If someone does give you a gift, do you feel compelled to return one to them?

When water is poured on a rock, it hits the rock and slides off. If water is poured onto a sponge, it is soaked up and then the soaked sponge can be used for other purposes. This is the way it is with love in relationships. Sometimes damage to our hearts distorts our view of love. We begin to believe that love is conditional and needs to be earned. If someone tries to give us love, we may push it away because we don't believe we deserve it. Because of this mentality, we will only pass on love if we believe those around us have earned it. This is actually not love at all.

In every relationship it is important to be able to receive love in order to give it. If our hearts are like a sponge, we can gladly receive the love others pass on to us as a gift. It isn't about whether or not we deserve it, but it really says something about the heart of the giver. When we question the motives of others out of a damaged filter system, we may tend to rationalize why they did what they did. If it is hard for us to receive, we will feel obligated to return the favor rather than receive their gift and enjoy it.

This is also very important in our relationship with Jesus. He gives us many gifts. If we only see them as given in proportion to our performance, we will keep trying to earn His love. Life is then about us and how good we are. If we can receive His gifts as part of His love for us, we can accept them with gratefulness and our eyes are turned toward the Giver. When we recognize them as gifts and absorb the love that was given to us, we will be able to readily pass on the gift of love to others--whether or not they earn it or deserve it.

PRAYER:

Lord, is my heart like a rock or a sponge? What is my motive in passing Your love on to other people? Do I do it to earn their favor or because I enjoy giving to them? Am I able to receive the gifts that You give to me, or do I try to earn them? Would You draw me a picture of my heart and how it responds to Your love? How does this affect the people around me? Is there anything in my heart that keeps me from accepting Your good gifts? If so, when did that get there? Is there a time in life that I began to believe that Your love needed to be earned? Would You heal my heart from that damage so that I can receive Your love?

Day 24

WHO IS SAFE?

"Fathers, do not irritate and provoke your children to anger (do not exasperate them to resentment), but rear them (tenderly) in the training and discipline and the counsel and admonition of the Lord."
Ephesians 6:4 (AMP)

"...Be an example to all believers in what you say, in the way you live, in your love, your faith, and your purity." I Timothy 4:12

"The name of the Lord is a strong fortress: the godly run to him and are safe." Proverbs 18:10

Some time ago our small dog, who was outside by herself for a few minutes, was attacked by a bigger dog. Our dog did not fair very well, coming away with broken ribs, many bruises and a possible collapsed lung. Thankfully, she lived. Prior to that happening, our dog was not afraid to be out by herself. After the traumatic incident, it was quite a while before she felt safe to go out. She was wary of it happening again. So it is with people after they have encountered a bad experience or trauma. Their ability to trust will be affected.

Safety...such an important aspect in relationships! People have asked the question as to how they can best help their children. One of my answers to them is "Be a safe place for them." We hear so many people talk about walking through life alone. No one was a safe place for them to talk about their difficulties. When people feel alone, they look for ways to fill that loneliness. This often leads them into greater difficulties.

Too often adults are unaware of how to be a safe place for children. A child may be curious, talkative, unthinking, innocent, and transparent, to name a few of the common characteristics of children. If a curious child is told he is too inquisitive, he will learn that it is not safe to ask questions. The talkative child may be told over and over to be quiet. The unruly child may be disciplined in anger. The transparent child may horrify his parents with his thoughts and imagination and be told to never think or talk about particular things. The innocent child may be punished when he has done nothing wrong. Then there are the times that a child disobeys. The adult may punish the child with anger and rigidity. When punishment is done in anger, fear will be created in the child. Consequently, he will feel unsafe with that adult. So often the punishment will be more for the convenience of the adult than for the training of the child. There are so many ways that a child may find himself feeling unsafe and unable to trust.

What would safety look like? What if gentleness, patience, and calmness would have been used toward the child instead of pressure to do things right? These qualities are all characteristics of what Jesus demonstrated to those around Him. What if there was no shock expressed when a child admitted a sin? What if there was encouragement instead of criticism? What if the adult listened to the talkative child, engaging in conversation with him? What if the adult challenged the curious child to keep learning more? What if the child knew his parent loved him after he was disciplined because of the kindness and gentleness expressed?

Many adults cannot trust because they have not known safety as a child. Trust cannot be demanded. Just as a child needs safety to learn trust, so does the child-heart of an adult. If they were damaged while young, it will take time. It isn't up to us to try to force them to trust. Our job is to show them a picture of who Jesus is through our responses and that He can be trusted. We can do that by consistently listening, caring, and being gentle regardless of their reactions. It is necessary to show patience and acceptance to them if we desire to see trust increase, leaving the growth to the Lord.

PRAYER:

Lord, am I a safe place for my children? In what ways might they be afraid to come to me? Am I a safe place for the adults around me? What do they experience from me? How would You like to change this?

Is there anybody, Lord, with whom I did not feel safe as a child? Am I still afraid of that same kind of pressure today? What made me afraid? Did You see that happen? What did You want to do with me when I was so afraid? How would You bring comfort to my hurting heart? Am I safe with You? Would You show me a picture of that safety?

Day 25

MY WORDS

"But no one can tame the tongue. It is restless and evil, full of deadly poison. Sometimes it praises our Lord and Father, and sometimes it curses those who have been made in the image of God." James 3:8-9

"Let's keep a firm grip on the promises that keep us going. He always keeps his word. Let's see how inventive we can be in encouraging love and helping out,....spurring each other on, especially as we see the big Day approaching." Hebrews 10: 23-25

I stand very distraught at the news of a friend
Who's been raped or robbed or defeated.
It makes me want to do all to defend
  This person so damage is no more repeated!

My mind can get twisted as it goes in a whirl
  "How can anyone get away with this!"
My anger builds and has intent to hurl
  Any words that would prove it injustice!

But wait...in <u>my</u> tongue lies the power of death or of life...
  My anger is about to destroy.
Am I any better than the one who caused strife
  With the thoughts and words I'm about to employ?

Who am I to think that I am better than they,
    When to those closest around I rebuke?
If I am upset, inconvenienced, or frustrated in a day,
    My defenses can arise like a duke.

I think I have right to criticize and blame
    Or give looks of unkindness to them;
With no thought of the "curse" that has power to lame
    Because I am out to defend and condemn.

These words DO have power to bring someone death
    And I've thought I am justified if crossed.
It can also happen by look or the sigh of a breath,
    Without thought of relationship that is lost!

"Lord, you've given me my tongue; it has power for evil or good.
    Help me to quit looking around,
But to look inward at what hinders the blessing that could
    Come from my mouth and abound.

Open my eyes to Yourself and to Who <u>You</u> are.
    I need Your grace <u>every day</u>!
Heal my heart and send the enemy afar
    So I experience Your character in a new way.

I desire for You to be the focus in each situation;
    The hammer on others and self I lay down.
Thank you for the blessing You've poured on me with passion;
    You are the God of LIFE so renowned.

Prompt me when my responses are not of You,
    And when I believe lies about me.
Teach me how to receive Your blessings full-brew
    So that Your LIFE overflows to others for FREE!"

This poem came out of a time I talked with Jesus about an inappropriate response I had toward Nevin.

PRAYER:

Lord, what kind of words have I been using toward myself? Are they blessing words or "cursing" words? What would You say about me? Why would I use destroying words about myself? When did that begin? Would You show me what that did to my heart? Would You show me what You do with my heart that has been damaged by words?

What kinds of words do I use toward those that are around me, Lord? Why do I do that? Would You draw a picture of what my words do to their hearts? Have You given me the ability to bless those around me? What would keep me from being able to do that? Would You show me how I could demonstrate Your character?

God's Grace Demonstrated in Strongholds

Day 26

FEAR OF FAILURE

"The godly may trip seven times, but they will get up again. But one disaster is enough to overthrow the wicked." Proverbs 24:16

"The Lord...delights in every detail of their lives. Though they stumble, they will never fall, for the Lord holds them by the hand." Psalm 37:24

Why is it that people fear failure? What does it mean about myself if I fail? I've come from a lifetime of being afraid of failure. This led to defensive reactions whenever someone corrected me in something. I thought it meant I was a bad person. Comments such as "You should know better" or "Why did you do *that*?" left me wondering if I had anything to offer to the world.

When we fear that we might fail, our focus is on ourselves and how successful we are. Some of us try very hard to succeed so we *won't* fail. The focus is on our own effort. Some of us give up because we *know* we won't succeed. When we do this, our focus is also on ourselves and our inabilities. It's easy to fall into the rut of having the final outcome determine whether or not we are a success or failure.

Is it really true that how well we do something determines who we are? What if we do the best we know how, but it still falls short of what we or others thought it should look like? Does that make us a failure? Is it possible that we are putting our focus on *doing* instead of on *being*? Is our value connected to our performance?

When we look at Jesus and the way He related to people, it is obvious that not everyone responded to Him positively. Look at Judas. He was a close disciple. His attitude toward Jesus was not good. Does that mean that Jesus didn't love him enough and was a failure at ministering to Judas? Absolutely not! Judas made his own choices. The final outcome of a situation does not determine whether a person is a success or a failure.

Jesus, not our success, is the determiner of our value. He values us 100% as infants. That value remains at 100% when we become 80 years old. Our value is not changed because we intentionally or unintentionally blow it. A friend, Allen Miller, made a statement something like this, "Failure does not happen when we fall. Failure happens when we refuse to get back up, clean up the mess and move forward." The Bible has much to say about people falling. The Bible also talks about victory. Victory is about Jesus and He values us enough to help us get back up and continue the journey with us.

When we look at ourselves as failures, we lose heart. We may often find ourselves unmotivated. We will also lose focus of the One who created us and His purpose for us. When we fall, let's reach out to His extended hand. He is ready and waiting to pick us up. He will offer comfort and tenderhearted correction that will allow us to live in VICTORY!

PRAYER:

Lord, it is so easy for me to focus on how I perform. I am often concerned about what people think. Why am I afraid of being a failure? Is there someone in my life that has made me feel that way? Do I try to prove myself to them? Have I given up being able to please someone? Jesus, when You look at me, do You see a failure? Would You draw a picture of what You see? What have I been believing about myself? What should I do when I find myself afraid of failure? Did You do enough to totally cleanse *me* from *my* failure? Thank You for Your cleansing power and freeing me from that bondage!

Day 27

THE HEAVINESS OF NEGATIVITY

"For I know the thoughts and plans I have for you, says the Lord, thoughts and plans for welfare and peace and not for evil, to give you hope in your final outcome." Jeremiah 29:11

"How precious are your thoughts about me, O God. They cannot be numbered!" Psalm 139:17

Have you ever had a friend who talked negatively about life? They were negative about themselves, about circumstances, and about other people. Did this kind of conversation have a negative influence on you?

I had a problem with negative thinking for much of my life. I was negative about who I was. I was negative about anything that interrupted my agenda. I was negative about what God allowed into my life. I was negative about all the negative happening around me. If people would give me compliments, I threw a negative comment back. I didn't like myself and it came out in my way of thinking and in my way of talking.

I have also been on the other side of the coin. I have heard other people be negative. At times I felt pressured to be negative just to be able to relate to them. Sometimes I've felt pressure to make sure that I do good or kind things for people to keep them from being negative.

Negativity puts tension in the air. It leads to depression. It can feel like there is a dark cloud around all the time. The negative or moody person may not even realize that they are negative; it is such a familiar place to live. Other people feel like they have to walk on eggshells so that the negative person doesn't get unhappy about one more thing. After they have been around negativity, people may go away feeling exhausted.

I know people have felt it from me, I've felt it from others, and I've heard many people express that they also have experienced it. It's a common problem. When it is a way of life and always has been, there is seemingly no way to turn that switch to the positive. We actually would feel like we were dishonest if we did.

If someone has negative thinking, there is a reason. At some point in time that person became very disappointed or hurt and nobody was there to care about their disappointment. This can happen very young in life and the person will live in that disappointment even though it is hidden deep within. Sometimes negativity is modeled by parents, teachers, or other adults, giving children the idea that is up to them to fix the adult's problem. Sometimes children believe that they are the reason the adults are unhappy.

The hardest part in my journey of healing has been the negative thoughts I had about myself. When I was able to go to Jesus as a child and put aside my adult rationalization, I saw that He cared and accepted me. My negativity about Him started to change. It was quite a journey of agreeing with Him about who I was. Eventually, I quit telling myself how hateful I was and how stupid I was. I am not sure when it happened. When I focused on not being negative, I became more negative. When I focused on Jesus and started to receive the things He said as truth, whether or not I felt them, His truth started sinking into my heart. Jesus gave me many pictures of what He thought about me and this was healing for me.

Over the years, my belief system has changed drastically. When I struggle with negativity, I can talk with Jesus about it and He offers comfort to my heart. It still is easy to see the negative happenings around me. The difference is that I also see the positive things. I also know that my negativity can wear on the people around me and I desire to be a safe place for people to interact. Negativity will only drain them or shut them down. Sometimes it takes time to process negative experiences, but I like to stay in conversation with Jesus about it until I come away agreeing with Him about Him, myself and others. In this way I can "take my thoughts captive."

PRAYER:

Lord, I have problems thinking negatively about so many things. When did negativity settle into my heart? Was there a huge disappointment to my heart that You would like to bring to my mind? What kind of message did I believe about myself? Did I make any promises or vows about myself when that happened? When You saw that my heart was so disappointed, what did You do? Why were You doing that? What was my heart longing for at the time? How would You like to show comfort to my hurting heart? What does negative thinking do for me? How does it affect those around me? Lord, I don't know how to help myself; I need Your help. What is one thing that You would like to say to my heart today? Would You keep talking with me about this in the coming days?

Day 28

WALKING IN FEAR

"Such love has no fear, because perfect love expels all fear. If we are afraid, it is for fear of punishment, and this shows that we have not fully experienced his perfect love." I John 4:18

"Trust in the LORD with all your heart; do not depend on your own understanding." Proverbs 3:5

The decision was made. I was moving from NW Ontario to Albuquerque, NM! Who would have ever thought such a thing would happen! I had always said I would NEVER move to a location where I knew no one. It was obvious that God was leading me this way, and I was surprised that I was willing to go. I was not going to Albuquerque because I had an obligation to obey God, but rather because I knew He was leading me there and I had assurance of His presence.

I was always a fearful person. I was afraid of people, afraid of the dark, afraid of storms, afraid of being alone, afraid of what people might think, afraid of failure...and much more. The life of fear has been very familiar to me. It was like walking in a maze with mile-high walls on either side and a roof over the top making it all dark. I was afraid of what was ahead. This fear paralyzed me, and I was unable to enjoy much of life because of all my fears. Since I lived with these fears so long, I just thought it was normal. People would make remarks to me like, "You don't need to be afraid," or

"Why would you be afraid of that?" I didn't know how to answer the questions, and neither could I just flip a switch to quit being afraid. Fear controlled my life and many of my decisions, which often kept me from venturing out of my comfort zone.

When I tried hard not to be afraid, I was never successful. Thus I knew I was a failure. When I focused on trying to trust, I would try hard. I wasn't successful at that either and ended up right where I always was--afraid. The enemy had done a good job of making me believe that I was created that way.

I'm not sure when things changed. As I understood that Jesus was not disappointed in me and that He cared about my fearful heart, I was drawn by His gentleness. The more I was drawn to Him, the more I trusted Him. He did not demand that I trust Him, He invited me. He did not condemn me for my fear, but rather pursued me and was patient.

Over the last number of years, I have found myself doing things that I never thought I would do. God has been breaking the chains of fear. As I have taken my focus off my fear and have begun to look for glimpses of Perfect Love (Jesus), I have been drawn to Him. The more I have experienced a personal relationship with Him, the more my trust in Him has grown. I understand more of His thoughts about me, and this has built more trust.

For me to move to Albuquerque was a big stretch. I was afraid. Because of my new relationship with Jesus, I asked Him for a picture of where He was on this journey. He showed me a picture of Him and I walking on a dirt road with a bend in it. He was going to protect me from the "bears," from the dark and anything else. He had a big flashlight so there would always be light even in the dark. He would not be leaving me! I asked Him what was around the bend. He said I didn't need to know that now, but He would show me when it was time. Even though there were many unknowns, my heart was comforted to walk into the future. Little did I realize He had many changes ahead, including marriage!

I still experience fear, but the fear doesn't have the control it once did. I'm thankful for those people who walked with me through the deep waters of understanding myself and my fears and gently turning me toward Jesus.

PRAYER:

Lord, I have a lot of fear. I've been trying for so long to get rid of it and it is not working. Is there another way? Would You draw me a picture of what You do when Your children are afraid? What is this fear doing to my heart? What caused this fear, Jesus? Is there an age or event You want to bring to my mind that would let me know when the fear began? How would You like to bring comfort to my fearful heart? When I find myself afraid, what would You invite me to do with that fear? What would You like to put in the place of fear? Would You restore my heart to the heart You created me to have?

Day 29

COMPARISON - A KILLER

*"...when they measure themselves with themselves and compare themselves
with one another, they are without understanding and behave unwisely."*
2 Corinthians 10:12b (AMP)

*"We do this by keeping our eyes on Jesus, the champion who initiates and
perfects our faith." Hebrews 12:2a*

Sometimes life seems like a race. We find ourselves distracted by the
people around us in an unhealthy way and our progress is hindered. It's
easy to allow these people and their thoughts to determine our value and we
can fall into the killer of comparison!

When we run the race of life with the comparison mentality, we will run in
ways that will hinder our progress. Sometimes we will find ourselves
carrying or juggling things in excess of our abilities. We may look at those
we think are ahead of us and try hard to keep up with them and their
accomplishments. We are driven to become like them. We may even
imagine what they might be thinking about us. These perceived thoughts
motivate us to prove to them that we are good or successful. Sometimes
these perceived thoughts slow us down. We become discouraged because
we don't believe we can ever achieve what we should. Then we see those
that are behind us. They ask us to help lighten their load so they can move
faster. We hate disappointing anyone, so we take on some of their

responsibilities. We become overwhelmed and find ourselves resentful and even critical of them. We start thinking what *they* should do to manage better. We're glad we are not quite as bad as they are. The race goes on. We look ahead and we look behind. We judge ourselves by looking at where they are. The longer we do this, the more daunting the race. Yet, some find it motivating. They are driven to stay in the lead to prove their success.

This mentality of life makes a person tired. It's all about how we perform. Our eyes are taken off the Author of our faith. We get sucked into thinking that the grass is greener on the other side of the fence. If we are single, we see all the wonders of being married. If we are married, we can see all the benefits of being single. If we have children, we wish for freedom and look at those without children and all the "time" they have. When we don't have children, we look at how fortunate those people are who have families. Comparison robs us of contentment.

What if our focus was on Jesus? What would it look like if we allowed Him to determine our value and who we are? Would we need to prove ourselves? Would we need to judge ourselves? Would we need to succumb to criticizing others to make ourselves feel good? What does our Creator, the One who knit us together, say about who we are? Do we believe Him?

PRAYER:

Lord, I have lost focus of You and have been distracted by those around me who are also running this race of life. Why am I drawn to do that? Would You draw me a picture of what I think about my own heart? Do I feel it necessary to meet up to the expectations of certain people? Who are these people? Why are they so important to me? Am I critical of people who don't think the way I do? How does criticism benefit me, Lord? When did I begin using this method of comparison and judgment? What do You think of me? Do I need to perform properly to please You? How are You different than those that I'm working hard to be like? Thank You for knowing my heart!

Day 30

I KEEP GETTING ANGRY, LORD

"And don't sin by letting anger control you. Don't let the sun go down while you are still angry." Ephesians 4:26

On this journey of healing for my heart, I became aware that I had inner anger toward myself. I always knew I had fear issues, but I really didn't struggle with anger that much--I thought. I had no idea that the negativity I had toward myself or my critical and judgmental attitude toward others were indicators of anger. I also had no idea that getting easily irritated was a close brother to anger. I just thought if people around me would be different, then I wouldn't have these problems. I figured it was normal to feel this way, but I didn't really like these things in my life. It didn't seem possible to get rid of them, so I was stuck. I was quite shocked when I realized these were all connected to anger.

Over time, as I began to agree with Jesus about myself, I could almost feel an ice cube in my heart melting away. The process was slow, but I began to get excited when I saw that some of these reactions weren't happening as often. It felt like God really was changing that inner anger and replacing it with acceptance toward myself and more acceptance and grace toward other people.

Then I got married. It had been many years since I lived in a common space with someone. I realized how much I had adjusted to living alone. Nevin didn't do things the way I did, and he didn't think like me. Even more devastating was the fact that he didn't always understand what my heart wanted or needed. My head knew that would be the case, but my heart was thinking it would "just fall into place." I was very disappointed to find my anger and criticism coming out at him occasionally. I thought I had dealt with my anger! Sometimes he would go quiet on me, or he would just leave the house when he knew I was upset. This triggered my rejection and I'd get more angry. I'm thankful these weren't daily occurrences, but it was more often than I liked.

One morning I was convicted of an angry response to my husband. I asked Jesus why I kept getting angry. He helped me realize that it happens when I feel like Nevin isn't listening to me or understanding me. I asked Jesus for comfort for my misunderstood and unheard heart. Then I asked Him what my anger did to Nevin. He showed me a picture of a jagged rock that was just the right size to throw. He said when I feel misunderstood, out of frustration I throw that jagged rock pretty hard at Nevin's heart. Nevin shuts down when he feels that rock. I never would have thought I would do a hurtful thing like that! Jesus did not condemn me for throwing the rocks, but suggested I buy a nerf ball from Walmart. When I feel frustration toward Nevin, I can throw the nerf ball at him. I told Nevin what Jesus had said and he was encouraged to know that I was working with this issue.

Sure enough, at a later time, I felt that frustration begin to rise. I realized I had a choice. I could throw my "jagged rock" or I could throw the nerf ball which was close by. I chose the ball. Nevin looked quite surprised when the ball came flying his way, but he caught on to the cue. We looked at each other and laughed, which broke the tension of the moment. He was able to understand what was creating my frustration and we talked out the issue without intensity on my part. God has continued to work in this area and I'm finding that anger and cutting remarks have lessened considerably.

When we recognize that our anger comes from a hurting heart, we can allow Jesus to heal that pain. Hurting people will hurt people. As we accept and experience His care for us, our attitude toward those around us becomes less demanding. As our hearts are healed by His comfort, attention and care, the sin we do from the damage in our hearts also is addressed.

PRAYER:

Lord, I find myself getting easily upset or irritated when people around me don't understand or cooperate with me. I get critical and place expectations on them. What happens to my heart when I feel misunderstood or disrespected? Are there other things that contribute to my anger, Lord? Would You draw a picture of my hurting heart when it is feeling those pressures? Are there lies I've been believing when it seems people don't care about me or my thoughts? What truths would You like to put in place of the lies? What do You do with Your children when they feel misunderstood? Would You show me what You would like to do with my damaged heart?

Lord, what does my anger do to those living around me? How would You like to change that? Would You draw a picture of what my anger does to their hearts? Is there forgiveness for me, Lord? What kind of messages am I passing on to my husband? My children? My coworkers? Could I give my anger to You? What would You like to put in its place? Thank You for Your healing and forgiveness.

God's Grace Demonstrated When Life Is Difficult

Day 31

LIFE IS OVERWHELMING!

"So teach us to number our days, that we may gain a heart of wisdom."
Psalm 90:12 (NKJV)

"Life is too busy!" "There's so much to do!" "I feel like I'm spinning my wheels!" "I'm living close to the edge!" These are comments that I've heard or have said in the hurry-scurry of life. At times I've become so overwhelmed because there is no time to just "BE!" Sometimes life seems insane and the future seems to hold no chance for respite.

What do we do with those times? Busyness seems to be a robber--of rest, of relationships, of "sanity," of peace, etc. It is even a robber of our personal relationship with Jesus. More than once I've heard statements like, "I was experiencing Jesus in special ways and then it fizzled out." After more discussion, it became apparent that a busy schedule had shifted the focus to surrounding circumstances. This led to discouragement.

I've been a master at feeling overwhelmed and frustrated in life. I've allowed the pressures of what I **should** do take control of my decisions and my emotions. When I focus on those "shoulds," my relationships take second place. My tone of voice tends to become sharper, my irritation level increases, and unexpected happenings in my day can become mountains. In my journey to finding God's healing for my heart, I'm finding there are other options outside of the old familiar path.

A few years ago we were heading into one of these very busy times. I knew myself and didn't really want to sacrifice relationships because of frustration and the inability to keep up emotionally. I decided it might be good to do some emotional preparation. I told Jesus about the upcoming events and asked Him what was happening in my heart. He showed me a picture of a messy egg salad sandwich. He said that He knew I liked egg salad sandwiches, but if they are squished and messy, I would tend to throw them away. I resonated with the picture as I knew I was ready to go AWOL with the upcoming trips and activities.

I asked Him what He wanted to do with that picture. He blew up the egg salad sandwich into one that looked fresh. He said the layers of bread represented the trips we were taking. The egg salad filling represented the busy week at home in between trips. The sandwich was fresh and looked appetizing. The upcoming activities were also things that I enjoyed doing; it was just way too much at one time. I asked Him what He wanted me to do with it. He suggested that I eat the sandwich one bite at a time and let each bite digest. He reminded me that when I eat bread too fast, I get the hiccups. I was amused; He was right.

I got the picture. For the next three weeks, I saw an egg salad sandwich in my mind each day. I would talk to the Lord about taking one bite at a time. Because of this help from Him, I did not find myself biting off the wrong things--like my husband's head. When the busy time was behind us, I was amazed that I had stayed quite sane! I thanked Him for His guidance through that process.

PRAYER:

Lord, life seems so busy and so overwhelming. I don't know which way to turn and I feel like I'm spinning my wheels. What would You like to do with my spinning heart? Is there something enjoyable You would like to show me about this day? From where are all the demands coming? Where are You today, Lord? How would You like to calm my heart as I face the demands around me? How much is my responsibility? How much is Yours?

Would You show me what it would look like to walk this day with You? What are You doing with the hearts of those closest to me? I ask for Your protection from the enemy who desires to rob me of peace during this busy time. Lord, would You bring a picture of peace to my heart?

Day 32

PEOPLE AROUND ME ARE HURTING

"The Lord is like a father to his children, tender and compassionate to those who fear him." Psalm 103:13

"The Lord is close to all who call on him, yes, to all who call on him in truth." Psalm 145:18

I couldn't sleep. My thoughts were constantly on an individual with whom I recently had had a conversation. The person was hurting. I wanted to help so badly. The desperation of the person made my heart feel heavy. What could I do?

As I talked to Jesus about this heaviness, I asked Him what I could do to help the person. He said to me, "Remember that time that you felt so desperate a few years ago?"

"Oh yes, I remember," I responded.

He replied, "You've never talked with me about that."

I thought a bit and realized He was right. So I asked Him where He was that one night when I felt so desperate with nowhere to turn.

He showed me a picture. He was in the closet. I asked Him what He was doing in the closet when I was needing to see Him. Then He said something that caught my attention. "Joann, you called out to Me. You wanted Me for what I could do to rescue you from your turmoil and desperation. You didn't want Me for Who I am. You had your own terms and what I should do for you. I was there all the time. I was with you; you just didn't see Me."

My eyes were opened. He had been there. I couldn't see Him because my eyes were looking only for what He should do for me. I was unable to experience Him for Who He was. This kept me in my pit of discouragement.

So I asked Him what that had to do with this friend. He said, "You have a hard time seeing people in desperation and hurt. Your caring heart doesn't like to see anyone desperate because you know how agonizing it can be. On the other hand, the pain from the desperation you experienced can drive you to convince people that they need to get out of their desperation. You will tend to put pressure on yourself to fix another person's problem and this pressure overflows onto them. You can only invite and leave the choice with them. Just as I was with you, so I am with your friend."

This brought me comfort. So I asked Him what my responsibility was to this person. He showed me a picture of the individual concentrating on the problem. Then I saw Him standing off to the person's side. He said to me, "This is between your friend and Me. All that person needs to do is turn and look at Me." Then I saw Him pull a curtain and I knew my friend was in good hands. Jesus was there.

This whole exchange brought peace to my heart. I was able to release the individual to Jesus and was once again able to sleep. I was unable to change the situation and I realized at that time, I was not that person's "savior." Jesus was. There will be times when those we love are hurting so badly and we want to help them. We need to allow them time to hurt and be their encourager and cheerleader instead of their rescuer. Our only job is to point them to Jesus.

PRAYER

Lord, there are people around me who are hurting so much. I want to help them. I hate to see them hurting all the time. Do You have any words of comfort for my heart? Is there anything You want to bring to my mind that he/she needs from me today? Would You draw me a picture of what You are doing with his/her heart today? What is my responsibility for this individual? What is Yours? When they come to my mind, what would You like for me to do? Would You draw a picture of how heavy my heart is because of this hurting person? What are You doing with my heavy heart? What would You like to put in place of the heaviness?

Day 33

I'M ALL ALONE

"I will never fail you. I will never abandon you." Hebrews 13:5

"...And be sure of this: I am with you always, even to the end of the age."
Matthew 28:20b

Have you ever been in a group of people and felt all alone? How can that ever happen? Loneliness is a common problem. It was very familiar to me most of my life.

What causes these times of deep loneliness? I don't have all the answers, but as I've contemplated the loneliness in my own life, I have some possibilities to offer. Is it possible that great loneliness comes from loss? This could be loss of something or somebody who was once a part of my life, or it could be loss of a desire that has never been fulfilled. These are legitimate reasons to feel lonely.

When loneliness overpowers a person, it has potential to affect the belief system about ourselves, about others, or even about God. It may often bring with it darkness and heaviness. We may begin to believe that if we were different, people would "be there" for us. The messages from the belief system may say that people don't care about us or even that if God cared, He would take away our loneliness and fill our longings. In the heat of our loneliness, we may demand that our longings should be filled in a certain way. We may become bitter at people or God. We may try to prove to ourselves and others that we are worth something. All these attempts actually drive people away from us, build fear inside of us, and produce more lonely feelings. Our passion in life focuses on being relieved of the loneliness. We tend to lose hope and faith in God. In this state, there really is nothing another person can do to relieve us of our problem. Time spent with people only provides a band-aid. Something deeper is causing the loneliness and we have been deceived into thinking it is caused by the people around us.

Is there any way that this can change? The more I understood the damage to my heart, I began to see my longings and desires as legitimate. Over time, I saw that I had unknowingly been demanding that God needed to fulfill my expectations before I could be happy. As I acknowledged and repented of this belief system, I learned that Jesus desired to bring comfort and healing into those longings if I would let Him. I recognized that Jesus had never been enough; I always thought people should be filling those holes. As I understood the misconceptions that came out of my hurt, I also recognized the lies I was believing about Jesus. Though the process was slow, my belief about Him began changing. Over time, the deep feeling of loneliness lessened.

This process of healing began happening even before I was married. Yes, I still felt it. Yet, I was much better able to accept my loneliness as an indicator of a longing rather than a belief about myself. The more I experienced Jesus on a personal level, the more I experienced His presence in my loneliness. My demands and expectations of other people decreased as a result. This allowed me to view my friendships as gifts from God rather than something to momentarily cover the emptiness inside. As I learned to accept that Jesus was enough for me, I believed He would never leave or forsake me. When I got married, it was not an escape from loneliness, but rather a gift that God brought to me!

Do I ever get lonely? Yes, there are times that I still experience it; however, it does not overpower my life like it once did. I recognize it more as a response to longings that I have. As I am able to give those longings or losses to Jesus instead of demanding that they be filled according to my desires, I find comfort from Him. Marriage has provided companionship and relationship in many new ways, but only Jesus can be the Healer for those longings and losses in life!

PRAYER:

Lord, are there areas in life where I feel all alone? Are these feelings of loneliness connected to longings of my heart or losses that I have experienced? Do You care about those, Lord? When did those longings first go unmet? What did I begin to believe about You? Would You draw me a picture of who I am to You? How would You like to bring comfort to my lonely heart?

Day 34

THE FIRE BURNS WILD AROUND ME

"'Look!...I see four men, unbound, walking around in the fire unharmed! And the fourth looks like a god!'...Not a hair on their heads was singed, and their clothing was not scorched. They didn't even smell of smoke!"
Daniel 3: 25, 27

"For we are not fighting against flesh-and-blood enemies, but against evil rulers and authorities of the unseen world, against mighty powers in this dark world, and against evil spirits in the heavenly places."
Ephesians 6:24

"But you, O Lord, are a God of compassion and mercy, slow to get angry and filled with unfailing love and faithfulness."
Psalm 86:15

There are times that individuals are in situations where they feel like they live in a hot fire. The people closest to them make it difficult to keep their focus on Jesus. They may have spouses who are very critical, angry, depressed, or detached. It gets wearisome living in this kind of environment. It seems there is no reprieve from the hot flames. It is not an emotionally safe environment and they can feel very alone.

God's grace is abundant for these individuals. Life may feel chaotic to them, full of tension and accusation. Is it possible to walk alone in the journey of healing for the heart, especially when the pressure is so continuous?

For the individuals who live in this difficult environment, there are two common reactions. They may become bitter at the hard-to-love individual around them and respond in anger, creating an evil-for-evil relationship. The other extreme is to try so hard to please the person, hoping to make them happy so the pressure is not so strong. Neither of these methods will work in bringing peace to the heart.

How did Jesus do it? He was constantly around criticism. Even his disciples did not understand who He was. He faced much anger and hostility as He walked this earth. Did He resort to bitterness? Did He retaliate? What made Him respond differently?

Jesus knew the heart of His Father toward Himself and toward other people. When we experience difficult people, it is easy to forget that they damage people out of their own hurting hearts. Jesus was able to keep His focus on the hearts of the people around Him. Jesus knew who He was to God, His Father. He allowed His Father to determine His identity. When we feel hard pressure from those around us, it is easy to let them determine our identity. We can feel like we are failures, we are stupid, we aren't needed, or we are worth nothing. We feel like we are walking in a hot-burning fire. We can forget who we are to God.

The people who live in the fire will need a support group who keeps directing them to the heart of the Father. They will need to be continually asking the Father what is their responsibility and what is not theirs to carry. They will need protection from turning toward bitterness and anxiety. It will be necessary to understand that their heart needs care from the Father, and it will be important that they can receive that care from Him in order to walk in agreement with Him.

PRAYER:

Lord, I feel like I'm living in the middle of an unending fire. The pressure of _____ is so strong and

I can't hold up under it any longer. Would You draw me a picture of my heart living under this pressure? Have I experienced this intense pressure any other time in my life? How would You show comfort for my heart today? Lord, have I done something to bring this on myself? How much of what is happening is due to his/her damaged heart? Would You draw me a picture of his/her damaged heart? What is my responsibility to it? What are You doing with his/her heart? Would You show me what You are doing with my heart today? Would You show me a picture of peace for today in the midst of the fire that is raging around me?

God's Grace Demonstrated Through Forgiveness

Day 35

THE BLANKET OF SHAME

"How precious are your thoughts about me, O God, they cannot be numbered!" Psalm 139:17

"For the Lord your God is living among you. He is a mighty savior. He will take delight in you with gladness. With his love, he will calm all your fears. He will rejoice over you with joyful songs." Zephaniah 3:17

Have you ever heard phrases like "Shame on you" or "You should be ashamed of yourself?" I've heard them and I've used them. When phrases such as those are used, what does that indicate to the recipient? If shame is a disgrace, are we honoring others by using those terms?

I grew up feeling very shameful about myself. I spent many years trying to work hard to get rid of it. Shame is an attack on "who I am" and is often so general and confusing that we don't know why it is there. It seems we can never get rid of it. I compare it to sticky slime. The more a person tries to get it off, the more it sticks. Shame robbed me of my identity and who Jesus made me to be. Shame manifested itself in various ways in my life. I was afraid to do many things because I knew I couldn't do them right. I knew this would affect how people would view me. Shame paralyzed me keeping me from talking with people, especially those I didn't know. Shame made me feel bad about myself, which caused me to put pressure on myself to be good. Because I worked so hard to be good, when I saw others doing things I thought were not good, I picked up the license to criticize them. This made me feel better about myself--for awhile.

Shame can often lead to a critical spirit. When we feel so bad about ourselves and cannot get rid of that "slime," we may try to pass it off onto others. To get out, we may end up comparing ourselves with others who, in our eyes, are more disgraceful. If we think they are better than us, we stay buried in shame. It can become a life of knocking ourselves or other people down.

When we are disappointed by people, we may rationalize that disappointment by placing shame on the ones who "should have known better." This places us in a little "higher" position. Life can become similar to playing King on the Hill--we work so hard to stay on top, yet we are so afraid of being pushed to the bottom. If we don't fight to be on top, we lay trampled on the bottom. Either way, the shame still sticks. This shame can keep us from experiencing a personal relationship with Jesus, because we feel so unworthy of His love. We may find ourselves unable to choose to receive it.

Thankfully there is an antidote for shame. Often shame does not disappear by confession of wrongdoing because it is an attack on who we are. One of the things I needed to do in ridding myself of shame was to view myself as a child going to Jesus. In this way I was able to see Jesus as an understanding, gentle person. As my heart began to trust His person, I talked to Him about my shame. I remember one time when He showed me that there was a blanket of shame wrapped around me causing me to suffocate. In my mind I saw Him lift the blanket from my face to allow room to breathe. This was probably the beginning of understanding how much shame had hindered me in my life. Later I remember having a picture of my heart being a closed up box that I was afraid to open. I didn't even know what was in the box but was afraid of it. Jesus asked me if He could shine His light in it to take a look inside. With much apprehension I gave Him permission. He opened the box and shone His light around. To my amazement He was not disgusted at me or disappointed in me. These are examples of times that I believe He used to remove shame from me--it wasn't too "sticky" for Him. As my view of Jesus changed, my view of myself began changing. As that changed, my view of others changed. My critical spirit about others lessened. I'm still on a journey in this area; He still is working with me. I'm so thankful for His gift of grace and the changing He has done so I don't have to hide in a box or suffocate.

PRAYER:

Lord, sometimes it is difficult for me to come to You because I feel so full of shame. Can I just come to You as a child? When did I begin to be afraid of You because of the shame? Why did I become afraid of what You would do or say? Would You show me what You think of me as Your child? Are You disappointed in me? Are there specific things I have done that have allowed shame to permeate my being? Are these things forgivable? Is there something that someone else has done or said to me that has heaped shame upon me? Does that shame have to stay there, Lord? Did You do enough on the cross to remove my shame? How have I been reacting out of shame? Have I been trying to get rid of that shame by myself? What would You like to put in its place?

Day 36

RELEASED FROM GUILT

"But if we are living in the light, as God is in the light, then we have fellowship with each other, and the blood of Jesus, his Son, cleanses us from all sin." I John 1:7

God gave us the gift of a conscience. If it is working properly, our conscience lets us know if we are doing right or wrong. If we do something wrong, it speaks deep inside of us and we feel guilty. This is actually a guide for helping us live life. Unfortunately, due to the damage to our hearts, legitimate guilt often gets confused with false guilt, or shame. Sometimes the conscience seems to work overtime or in some cases, it becomes seared.

Guilt comes because we have done something wrong. When we feel guilt, it is actually a blessing. If we are unsure of what we did, we can ask God and He will show us. He speaks specifically and there is clarity. We then can confess the wrongdoing to Him and make it right with any other people involved. When we confess our wrongdoing to God, He has a whole unlimited storehouse of forgiveness to offer us. Because of the blood that was shed on the cross, we are clean before Him if we accept this gift of forgiveness!

Often one of the hardest steps is to forgive ourselves. We keep punishing or pressuring ourselves to "pay" for our sin by our performance. Forgiving ourselves is really just agreeing with God about ourselves. Forgiveness is all about His goodness! If He says that I am clean before Him, He would like for me to receive His free gift and enjoy it. When we do this, we can enjoy what He's done for us and our hearts are freed from bondage. We can live as victors!

There are times that we may feel false guilt. We don't even know what we did; there is a vague feeling that we must have done something wrong. Another person's unhealthy reaction makes us question ourselves. We try to figure it out, but there is nothing specific. Sometimes we go to the person and apologize just in case we did something. The guilt just won't go away. The false guilt, like shame, lingers and sticks to our being. It is from the enemy who speaks in generalities and is nagging. He can be sent away. The sense of false guilt or shame will often not be lifted by asking for forgiveness. We don't even know what we did to need forgiveness! We can ask the Lord where the guilt began. We can ask Him if another person's reaction placed this guilt/shame on us. God is not accusing and He is not elusive, but He is all about cleansing and forgiving. If we have done wrong, He will be delighted to gently show us where we erred. We can always be cleansed of our wrongdoing and do not need to live in that guilt. When it lingers, that can be a sign that we have either not forgiven ourselves or that we are struggling with false guilt. Instead of forgiveness, our hearts will need comfort, assurance and healing from the pain that caused it.

PRAYER:

Lord, is my heart living in guilt for something I did wrong? Have I accepted Your forgiveness for that or have I been trying to earn it? Thank You for your forgiveness for my wrongdoing. Am I living in agreement with You about my sin? Has it been completely forgiven? Am I clean before you, Lord?

Have I been carrying false guilt and blaming myself for someone's hurtful reactions? Would You show me what they did to my heart? Would You heal my damaged heart that was hurt by _____? How would You lift that heavy load? What would You like to put in its place?

Day 37

THE POISON OF BITTERNESS

"Look after each other so that none of you fails to receive the grace of God. Watch out that no poisonous root of bitterness grows up to trouble you, corrupting many." Hebrews 12:15

"Anxiety in the heart of man causes depression, but a good word makes it glad." Proverbs 12:25 (NKJV)

For many years I struggled with a lot of negative thoughts. I had negative thoughts about who I was as well as about life in general. This negativity was very familiar. As I grew older, the negativity was also toward the people around me. This resulted in a critical spirit. I had a lot of fear and anxiety. Due to the negativity about myself, I was anxious about being acceptable to others. I was anxious about my acceptance to God.

Over the years, the emotional load became too heavy to carry. This resulted in depression. Eventually I lost motivation for even the things I enjoyed doing. Life was very dark. I needed some outside help to walk with me through this deep valley. I was shocked when it was suggested that I had bitterness inside. I didn't think I was an angry person. Bitterness was a serious sin. I couldn't have bitterness! Yet, as I began to realize what bitterness really was, it was evident that I had the disease. It was poisoning my heart. I lived many years wishing life would be different, wishing people would be different, and wishing I would be different. I would often hear that when one feels this way, they should just think about the positive things and be grateful. They should reach out to others instead of being so stuck on themselves. I didn't know how to think in a positive way. I tried hard to be thankful and reach out to others. But, the turmoil inside remained.

Negative thinking, a critical spirit, defensiveness, and the tendency to get upset over seemingly small disappointments were all signs of bitterness. I always just figured that was who I was. After all, the personality tests said those would be my weakness.

Until I came to the place that I admitted there was bitterness, I saw no need to work with it. I was able to forgive only to the depth that I was able to recognize that I was hurt. Instead of trying to get rid of the symptom of depression, my counselors led me to examine the areas where my heart was hurting. I began understanding why I felt so confused and disappointed about life. I was led to talk with Jesus about those times, the people involved, and about myself. There were times I needed to ask Jesus where He was and if He cared. There were times I needed to release the people who hurt me. There were times I realized I was putting on others or myself the same pressures that I had experienced. I began to see that I was capable of hurting other people even if it was not my intent. When I experienced the grace that Jesus had for me, my grace for other people grew. Though I cannot put my finger on a specific place or time, slowly the bitterness within lessened. My awareness of how much Jesus loved me began to increase, and my negative thoughts about myself were less. My critical spirit toward others greatly decreased. Interestingly, my depressive spirit also began to lift. I began to see light at the end of a dark tunnel.

I don't know when it all happened. I describe it more as a "stepping stone" time. As I took one step at a time, Jesus did a little more healing. It wasn't until I was quite a distance down the path that I could look back and see I was at a different place than ever before! The ability to receive Jesus' love became my antidote for bitterness. Out of His love, He could heal my heart and I was able to release the people that had been held hostage in my heart. My ability to agree with Him about myself and about the people around me increased over time.

PRAYER:

Lord, is there any bitterness in my heart? Is there a negative experience that happened to me in the past onto which my heart is holding? Why can't I seem to loosen my grip? What damage was done to my heart by that experience? Would You draw me a picture of where You were when it happened and what You were doing? How would You like to bring comfort and peace to my heart? What messages were connected to my heart because of that painful experience? Would You connect the truth to my heart and disconnect the bitterness? How would You take that poison out of my system? What else would You like to tell me today?

Day 38

LIVING IN FORGIVENESS

"Instead, be kind to each other, tenderhearted, forgiving one another, just as God through Christ Jesus has forgiven you." Ephesians 4:32

"That's what my heavenly Father will do to you if you refuse to forgive your brothers and sisters from your heart." Matthew 18:35

"Lord, how often should I forgive someone who sins against me? Seven times? 'No, not seven times,' Jesus replied, 'but seventy times seven.'" Matthew 18:21-22

There was a lot about forgiveness that I did not understand. I thought I knew how to forgive. Basically, if someone apologized, I was quick to tell them it was nothing and extend my forgiveness. Then it was all over. I never knew that my negative feelings about life might have to do with a lack of forgiveness. I was a believer trying to do right and I knew that I needed to forgive to receive forgiveness. Had anyone suggested that I had a forgiveness problem, I would have denied it.

One of the ways I learned to cope was to deny I had been hurt! Unfortunately, my forgiveness went only as deep as I would admit that I was hurt. It was quite a long journey to understand that my heart was hurting. It was an even longer journey to understand that my heart was also bitter, which produced the negativity about myself and about other people.

I was also angry at God for not rescuing me from the difficult things in life.

Forgiveness from the heart has been a process. First I needed to admit there was hurt or I couldn't have been led to forgive from the heart. Then I needed to be willing to accept responsibility for the emotional pain I had experienced and the consequences of that pain. This meant that I would need to choose to do something with my hurting heart. It needed healing. It needed comfort. To expect the people around me to change would mean that my healing would be dependent on them. I needed to release the people from being what I wanted them to be and accept them as they were. My heart needed comfort, but that comfort would need to come from Jesus instead of from the people around me. It took time for me to allow Jesus to comfort my heart. At times, I didn't believe I deserved the comfort. At other times, I didn't believe that the comfort of Jesus was enough; I wanted understanding from the people who had hurt me. It was a big hurdle to get through. The more I allowed Jesus to comfort my heart, the more willing I was to release the people who hurt me, leaving them into God's hands. My heart eventually released the grip it had on them.

As I learned to allow Jesus to take care of my heart, I was actually extending a favor to those who hurt me. I was freeing them from the responsibility of taking care of my heart, and I was releasing them from understanding me fully. I could not comfort myself, but Jesus could. He demonstrated this in many ways.

As Jesus continued ministering to my heart, I was able to see that the bondage of my negativity hindered me from living out of the heart He gave me. I gave the ground of my heart back to Jesus that the enemy had stolen through bitterness and hurt. I gave Him permission to use that ground for His purposes.

Just because I forgave once did not mean that I never had negative thoughts and bitterness again. It has been necessary to continue forgiving "seventy times seven." When my heart feels hurt, instead of holding on to the hurt and acting out of it, I try to immediately talk to Jesus about what happened. I try to stay in conversation with Him until my heart experiences His comfort and I am able to release the individual into His hands. It is not necessary for me to make sure the individual knows they hurt me. It is necessary that I come to the place of allowing Jesus to be the comforter to my heart regardless of whether the individual is even aware of the hurt or verbally admits it.

PRAYER:

Lord, is my heart full of negativity about anyone? Am I believing that someone else needs to change so that I can be happier? Am I holding on to that individual and letting them control me? What damage did they do to my heart, Jesus? How would You like to bring healing to it? Would You like to draw me a picture of their heart? Am I holding on to it or am I ready to let You have that heart? Lord, I give You their heart. They do not need to change in order for my heart to be healed. I will allow You to heal my heart instead of depending on them to understand. In the coming days when I face that pressure again or when I face that person, what would You like me to do? Would You draw me a picture of Your involvement with me? If they hurt me again, would You remind me to bring my heart to You for healing?

Day 39

FORBEARING ONE ANOTHER

"With all lowliness and meekness, with longsuffering, forbearing one another in love;" Ephesians 4:32 (KJV)

"Always be humble and gentle. Be patient with each other, making allowance for each other's faults because of your love." Ephesians 4:32

"Love never gives up, never loses faith, is always hopeful, and endures through every circumstance." I Corinthians 13:7

There was a time that I became frustrated when people would talk about being forbearing or overlooking other people's faults. It felt like they were wanting me to pretend that there was no problem with what was happening and just "shove it under the carpet." I had the assumption that it meant that one shouldn't talk about it or even remember that it happened. It felt like I had to be dishonest, and this was confusing to me.

I often hear individuals talk disgustedly about people who are close to or not-so-close to them. They believe their critical spirit is justifiable. Their attitude indicates that the other person really needs to get their act together. I've heard people respond this way about the ugly things in family members, in children, in church-goers, etc. I have been guilty of the same thing. If we were to forbear instead with these unloving people, what would that look like? Does it really mean just pretending nothing happened?

137

The Bible talks about forbearing with one another in love. All people are going to do unloving things at times. There have been times when I tried to help people when I unintentionally hurt them. They misinterpreted my motives or I misunderstood their needs. Then there are those times that I have gotten defensive and I hurt people out of my self-focus. People with whom I interact will likely hurt me at times, whether intentional or not. What will I do with them?

To forbear means to endure. That is what Jesus did. He saw the sins of the people. He saw the disciples and their selfishness, their arguing, their humanness. Yet He accepted them right where they were. His relationship with them remained most important. When we view people through the eyes of Jesus, our response to them will be softer. We will be able to think the best about them instead of believing that their intent is always wrong. At times I can find myself unhappy with something that a person said or did. When I ask myself if I really believe they intended to come across in a hurtful manner, I can better control my reactions. Even if their intent was to hurt, I have Jesus who can offer comfort to me. When I take this approach, I am better able to accept them as they are without dwelling on the negative things.

People long to be understood and accepted. One of the best ways to put this into practice is to forbear. This would mean overlooking the unloving acts that they do and believe the best about them. Rather than pretending, it is admitting that their actions don't feel good. Because I have Jesus who is my comfort, I can look at their heart and love them in spite of what they did.

PRAYER:

Lord, is there someone that I have a hard time accepting? Is there anyone that I have negative reactions or a critical spirit toward? What would keep me from overlooking their faults? Do I feel threatened by them? If so, why would this be? Would You draw me a picture of what forbearing in love would look like? What does my heart feel from this person when they do those unloving things?

How would You like to bring peace to my heart? Am I struggling to release this person to You? Would You show me how to do that in the coming days? Would You show me a picture of that person's heart? What do You think of them? Would You teach me how to love and believe in this person? Would You open the eyes of my heart to see them as You see them?

God's Grace Demonstrated Through Encouragement

Day 40

THE FITBIT

"Come to me, all you who are weary and carry heavy burdens,
and I will give you rest. Take my yoke upon you.
Let me teach you, because I am humble and gentle at heart,
and you will find rest for your souls.
For my yoke is easy to bear, and the burden I give you is light."
Matthew 11:28-30

Recently I purchased a Fitbit. This is a step tracker plus a few more things. I can put this gadget around my wrist and forget about it. The handy little app on my phone tells me the results of my activity each day. I do nothing to make the Fitbit work except to make sure it is charged; it does what it was intended to do. Even when I'm not in touch with what it's doing, it is recording data that I can access on the app at any time. Though I'm not consciously aware of it every minute of the day, I'm very aware of it running in the subconscious. Occasionally I give it a couple taps to see my progress. The tangible results motivate me to stay more active. Whenever I wish, I can go to the worldwide web and get a few more details about my activity. It even tracks my sleep, which is kind of interesting.

As I was thinking about the Fitbit one day, my mind wandered to my emotional/spiritual life. What keeps me interested in preserving my health in those areas? What could I "purchase" that would help me track my "steps" with Jesus. What would help keep me in sync with my heart and what is happening? I asked Jesus what would be a spiritual Fitbit. Immediately Matthew 11:28-30 came to mind. I began pondering about the similarities between the Fitbit and this verse from Jesus.

1 - I can carry it with me every moment of the day.

2 - Just as the Fitbit helps in exercise and promoting weight loss, practical application of these verses will help to remove excess weight—if I let them motivate me and latch onto them in a tangible way.

3 - Jesus is offering to be my emotional/spiritual Teacher; my job is come to Him and He will give me the "data"(my yoke) that I need to know.

4 - If I want to find out more information about certain aspects of my journey, I can go to a "web" - His Word for encouragement, His arms for comfort, His presence for communication, etc.

5 - Even though I may forget occasionally that I am wearing this "Fitbit," my subconscious can be well aware of His presence.

I get excited the more I process the possibility of a spiritual tracker because I like tangible motivations. These verses can become reality, and the greatest thing about it is that it's FREE! I can get the benefits just by coming to Jesus! He has offered to be my trainer and teacher! He is gentle and knows how much I can handle and what is going to be beneficial for me. Too often I forget to put on my "Fitbit" and I become my own "trainer." I make my own decisions. I let others influence my decisions rather than first taking my heart to Jesus and asking Him what His "yoke" is for me that day. No wonder I become weighted down!

PRAYER

Jesus, how would You like to minister to my heart today? Would You like to be a part of each step I take? What is the first thing You invite me into for this day? What kind of exercise would You like to do with me? Is there a part

of my day that is MY plan, and not YOURS? I invite You to prompt me to "tap" into You today. Thank you for being my gentle Trainer and for the rest I can find when I choose to "exercise" in sync with You!

Day 41

THE MOUNTAIN CLIMB

"So let's not get tired of doing what is good. At just the right time we will reap a harvest of blessing if we don't give up." Galatians 6:9

"...Because of the joy awaiting him, he endured the cross, disregarding its shame. Now he is seated in the place of honor beside God's throne." Hebrews 12:2b

"He renews my strength. He guides me along right paths, bringing honor to his name. " Psalm 23:3

With anticipation I looked at the mountain looming in front of us. This was the mountain my siblings and I chose to climb. We had been talking about this challenge for several days and here we were! I started out with vim, vigor and vitality.

There was no trail to follow. It was all Alaskan tundra; you could walk anywhere. We were focused on our goal--the summit! I had just come from a year of teaching school. My body was not prepared for this kind of a trek, but I was healthy. I knew I could make it.

My outlook began changing about half way up. No longer did I experience much enthusiasm. The summit seemed illusive and unreachable. My aching muscles convinced me I wasn't fit for this task. I wanted to go back to the comfort of the vehicle. My motivation was decreasing very fast. Discouragement settled in. Seeing the summit was not for me, I finally told the group that I would sit and wait. I was too tired to keep going! I was disappointed in myself, but I didn't have what it took to reach the top.

I sat about ten minutes or more. Suddenly my sister called to me to come see a dall sheep! It was just a bit further up the mountain. I got up and followed her. I wanted to see the sheep if it was close by! As we neared it, it moved a little higher up the rocky mountain. We followed it to try to get more glimpses. We saw several of them. Before long, I looked up. We were close to the top. The dall sheep had taken my eyes off the laborious task ahead and had given me enjoyment as I made the climb. That day, I saw the summit of the mountain in all of its beauty.

So it is with the journey of healing. We get started on a path, but it uses different "muscles" and takes us out of our familiar way of living and believing. When we focus on our progress, we can get discouraged. We wonder why we do the same things over and over. Why aren't things changing?! It's easy to lose hope of achieving our goal. We compare ourselves with others. We wish it would be easier. We are tempted to go back to the old way. Yet we've come so far and really do anticipate a new view.

Just as God brought deliverance for Joseph, a raven for Elijah, and a dall sheep for me, He will bring encouragement to you! Look around. What does He want you to focus on that will move you toward the summit? This path of healing is a journey. It takes one step after another--sometimes smaller and sometimes bigger. Sometimes we need to go backward before we can keep moving forward. The view at the summit is worth the journey! Keep traveling on!

PRAYER:

Lord, the journey is hard! I get so discouraged with all the setbacks. I guess I thought it would be easier. Jesus, is there any hope for me? Do You care about my discouraged heart? How would You like to bring refreshment to my heart today? Where has my focus been? How would You like to shift that focus, Lord? Do

You see me as a failure? What do You see when You look at me? Would You bring me a picture of victory instead of failure? What one thing would You like me to think about today that would help me keep trudging upward?

Day 42

THE REMODELING PROCESS

"But those who trust in the Lord will find new strength. They will soar high on wings like eagles. They will run and not grow weary. They will walk and not faint." Isaiah 40:31

"The Lord gives his people strength. The Lord blesses them with peace." Psalm 29:11

Excitement was in the air. The time for closing had come for our new house! We received the keys and were able to walk through the place. The occupants had moved out and it was OURS! We saw purpose for the place, we had vision for it, and we were excited about all the possibilities. It was a solid structure, it had the criteria for which we had specifically prayed, and there were even some extra blessings that came with the house.

With the "new" house came some remodeling. The place smelled like smoke. Carpets were stained. Everything would need a new coat of paint. The kitchen and one wing of the house were going to need to be remodeled to make it more useable for our purposes.

We took two weeks off work thinking that we should be able to get quite a bit done on the house. We had a lot of neighborly volunteer help. At the end of two weeks, we were a long way from moving in. In fact, by that time, the house was in worse shape than when we bought it. In the remodel process, things seemed to take longer than we expected. Things didn't always go according to our plans. Instead of a couple weeks, it took a couple months! During that time, I found myself having a wide range of emotions. In the beginning there was excitement and vision. As the days drug on, the excitement slowly was replaced with drudgery, impatience, and disappointment. At times I wondered if the remodeling would EVER be finished. We eventually did move in, but not when we had hoped to and even then we have continued to upgrade throughout the years we have lived here.

Because we took the time to remodel, we have a much nicer home than if we would have bypassed the mess and settled in as it was. We are now enjoying the fruit of our labor that at one point seemed so endless.

This is similar to emotional healing. Life is a journey. I've experienced it and have heard others express their impatience in the process. We want instant changes rather than going through the remodel stage. We forget that we are learning new patterns of thinking and they don't come automatically. Sometimes we forget what tools we have available. There are times we get too tired to pick up the tools that are at our disposal and it's easier to just go back to the way it was. The changes we do see are slow and we get disheartened. We thought that when we decided to make the changes, life would be easier. We lose vision of what God has shown us.

When I am reminded by friends that I am normal, I am encouraged. This is a journey and it's normal to become fatigued in the journey. This reminder gives me strength to continue on. I tend to forget that I am in the process of a "remodeling." Sometimes the "remodel" job is bigger than at other times. We are in process and the outcome of God's working in our hearts is worth the effort!

PRAYER:

Lord, I've become impatient with what is going on in my life. I've been wanting the change to happen quickly and it's hard to keep on when I don't see anything happening. Jesus, what do You see in me? It seems I keep falling

back into my old patterns. Is there something that is causing me to do that? Are You disappointed in me, Lord? I need Your strength to continue on. I can't do it alone. My strength is so limited, and the journey ahead seems so long. How would You like to encourage my heart today, Lord?

Day 43

WHERE DO I GO FROM HERE?

"We will not hide these truths from our children; we will tell the next generations about the glorious deeds of the Lord, about his power and his mighty wonders." Psalm 78:4

"Jesus Christ is the same yesterday, today, and forever." Hebrews 13:8

"So let us come boldly to the throne of our gracious God. There we will receive his mercy, and we will find grace to help us when we need it most." Hebrews 4:16

Well, you have reached the end of the book! Now what? Just as this book has an unexpected number of chapters, so life is not always predictable. I hope you've recorded how God has been working. Life will go on and so does God's grace. Things will come up. Jesus Christ remains the same, yesterday, today, and forever. Keep conversing with Him. Relax and enjoy His presence. Delight in the things He has shown you about Himself, about you, and about other people.

I encourage you to reread the things that God has been showing you because we tend to forget. Find someone who is safe to whom you can verbalize the nuggets. The enemy has more power when we carry things alone. As we share with people, we can hear ourselves testify of God's goodness. This also builds strength.

Sometimes the damage is too difficult and we need someone to walk with us through the dark valleys. Don't be afraid to seek outside help. There are offices around the US and Canada that use the concepts talked about in this book. You may want to check out www.caringfortheheart.com to discover more information about Caring for the Heart and options for further help.

I am thankful for the impact that Caring for the Heart has had on my journey to emotional healing. I'm still on the journey. Things still resurface. After all, my past won't change, but what I allow God to do with my past can change. He doesn't waste pain! He desires to heal that pain so I can pass on His comfort to others. I'm thankful for those who have walked with me and have been a picture of Jesus. This life is really about Him!

God has been so gracious to me. I am learning to enjoy life much more fully and I am still learning more. I understand better what my choices are when things get rough. I still blow it, but He helps me back on my feet. I still get discouraged at times, but He provides encouragement. It doesn't take as long as it once did to change my perspective about things. I am grateful that He is still in the healing business. God is gracious!

PRAYER:

Thank You, Lord, for the healing You have been doing in my life. What is one thing for me to focus on for today? What would it mean to relax in Your love? How would You like to encourage my heart today? How could I encourage others? Thank You for walking with me and showing me more about who You are and about the mighty ways in which You work!

SUGGESTED RESOURCES

If you have found this book helpful in any way, you may be interested in some other valuable resources. The following resources present additional practical principles of the Caring for the Heart model of Biblical counseling.

- Biblical Concepts Counseling Workbook

- Caring for the Emotionally Damaged Heart Workbook

- A Practical Guide to the Caring for the Heart Model of Prayer

These, along with other resources, are available from:

Caring for the Heart Ministries
Colorado Springs, Colorado
email: caringfortheheart@msn.com
719-572-5550

OR

Online from Biblical Concepts Distribution
www.biblical-concepts.com

ABOUT THE AUTHOR

Joann Nisly spent 24 enjoyable years in Christian School ministry in NW Ontario. In 2007, God led her to move to Albuquerque, NM, where she met Nevin Nisly and his five adult children. She and Nevin were married in 2008. A year after their marriage, they moved to Partridge, KS, with a desire to be involved with Biblical counseling. They had completed their internship with Caring for the Heart Ministries just prior to moving. Nevin and Joann established a counseling ministry out of their own home, HOPE Ministries of KS, in 2010 using the Caring for the Heart model of Biblical counseling. They are currently full-time in this nonprofit ministry. Joann's desire to help others experience the grace of God in their hearts came out of her own difficult journey through depression. More information about the ministry can be found at www.nislysHOPEministries.com.

Joann enjoys spending time with their ten grandchildren whenever she gets the chance. She also enjoys doing life with Nevin. Together they enjoy walking with people on their emotional journeys, playing board games, doing gardening, playing tennis, traveling, and interacting with family. Joann is grateful for the healing God has brought into her life and is excited about seeing others experience the same for themselves.

Made in the USA
Columbia, SC
19 April 2018